AND I WILL
BE FOUND
BY YOU

AND I WILL
BE FOUND
BY YOU

FRANCIS FRANGIPANE

Copyright © 2009 Francis Frangipane

Published by Arrow Publications, Inc.
P.O. Box 10102
Cedar Rapids, IA 52410
www.arrowbookstore.com

Printed in the United States of America

Second Printing, October 2011

ISBN 978-1-886296-55-8

CONTENTS

Part Three: The Great Pursuit: Christlikeness

Part Four: Becoming a True Worshiper

Please Note:

Fifteen of the twenty-five chapters in this edition were originally published in previous books by Pastor Frangipane. These particular chapters were actually written over a span of twenty-seven years. They were selected because of their consistency with the theme of this book. Like the scribe who "brings out of his treasure things new and old" (Matt. 13:52), we felt these messages added a depth to this study on seeking God. It is our prayer that, together with the ten new chapters, the message of this book will bring added substance to your already inspired life.

INTRODUCTION

I can honestly say I feel I've been writing this book my entire adult life. This was not the case with any of my previously published themes. The books on spiritual warfare or church unity, or even the vision of attaining Christ's likeness, all came further down the path. However, the reality of seeking God has been different. The fabric of this truth has been woven into my spiritual life since I first came to Christ in 1969.

Perhaps, it is because my inherent skills are generally average that I am frequently compelled to seek God's help. In this regard, my insufficiencies serve me well. But, beyond my frequent need of divine intervention, I have also hungered to truly know the Lord. I believe that the real goal of Christianity is not to create a religion about God, but that we would actually know Him, experiencing firsthand the wonders and power of His incomparable life.

Thus, I have discovered that each time I seek the Lord, the deliberate movement of my heart toward Him leads me into far more than a simple answer to my need. In seeking God, I actually find Him. I reconnect with the living One – my rescuer, my redeemer, and the restorer of my soul. I have an answer, but I also have an ally whose wisdom is all-encompassing and whose incalculable power can transform all things with just the look of His gaze.

As I look at many in the church who are pining away spiritually, it is obvious to me: the great need of Christians is for more of God. Even as the psalmist wrote, "God has looked down from heaven upon the sons of men to see if there is anyone who understands, who seeks after God" (Ps. 53:2).

Seeking God – possessing a heart after God – this is the key that unlocks everything.

—FRANCIS FRANGIPANE

PART ONE

ALL WE NEED IS MORE OF GOD

When You said, "Seek My face,"
My heart said to You,
"Your face, O Lord, I shall seek."

—PSALM 27:8—

ONE

THE TENT OF MEETING

There are certain times when the Lord calls us out of the routine of our daily lives. These are special seasons where His only command is, "Seek My face." The Lord has something precious and vitally important to give us that the familiar pattern of our daily lives cannot accommodate. During such times, people are often delivered of sins that have plagued them for years; others discover a new depth in their walk with God and, thus, greater effectiveness in ministry and prayer. Still others obtain breakthroughs for their families and friends as the Lord, in response to their drawing near to Him, brings their loved ones into His kingdom.

Many times we expect spiritual breakthroughs to occur automatically, but most things we obtain from Heaven arrive via our asking, seeking, and knocking. In other words, we have not because we ask not. Pursuing the Lord is the secret to a fulfilled life.

Recall the words of King David. He was a man who was forced to live in the wilderness; he was hunted by enemies and slandered throughout the nation by King Saul and his cohorts. David had many reasons to fear, yet instead he lived boldly. Where did David's confidence come from? He said, "I sought the Lord, and He answered me, and delivered me from all my fears" (Ps. 34:4).

David wasn't delivered from "all [his] fears" simply in the routine of life's course. No, he said, "*I sought the Lord* ... and He ... delivered me." When we seek God, our faith is restored. As we draw near to the fullness of God, our fear is subdued.

HIGHEST GOAL IN SEEKING GOD

Those who understand the ways of God know that many of the greatest realities God has for us are gifts He has hidden in His heart. To obtain these blessings, God must be sought. You see, the Lord not only desires to bless us, He wants us to draw near to Him. He wants us to discover and know His deep love for us.

Thus, the highest form of seeking God is not for personal needs or even for other people. There comes a time when we seek God for Himself. Maturity comes as we break the cycle of seeking God only during times of hardship. A touch from God is wonderful, but we are in pursuit of more than just an experience – more than "goose bumps and tears." We are seeking a place of abiding in Christ, where we are keenly aware of His presence within us.

How do we enter this sacred place? If we will study the life of Moses, we see how he sought God and lived in fellowship with Him.

> Now Moses used to take the tent and pitch it outside the camp, a good distance from the camp, and he called it the tent of meeting. And everyone who sought the Lord would go out to the tent of meeting which was outside the camp.
> —Exodus 33:7

Notice that "everyone who sought the Lord would go out." If we are going to truly seek the Lord, we must "go out" as did Moses and those who sought the Lord. We must pitch our tent "a good distance from the camp." What camp is this? For Moses, as well as for us, it is the camp of familiarity.

Is there anything inherently wrong or sinful about the things that are familiar? No, not in themselves. But you will remember that when Jesus told His disciples to follow Him, He called them to leave the familiar pattern of their lives for extended periods and be alone with Him (Matt. 19:27). Why? Because He knew that our human nature is unconsciously governed by the influences of the familiar. If He is to expand us to receive the eternal, He must rescue us from the limitations of the temporal.

This is not to say that we neglect our families or become irresponsible as we seek God. No. But if we set our priorities right, we will discover that God has given everyone enough time to seek Him. After having done what love would have us do for our families, we simply say "no" to every other voice but God's. We redeem our time: cancel hobbies, forsake television and the Internet, put away the newspaper and magazines. Those who truly desire to find God – find time.

Beyond Just Normal

Many Christians have no higher goal, no greater aspiration, than to become "normal." Their desires are limited to measuring up to others. Without a true vision of God, we most certainly will perish spiritually! Paul rebuked the church at Corinth because they walked "like mere men" (1 Cor. 3:3).

God has more for us than just becoming nicer people; He wants to flood our lives with the same power that raised Christ from the dead. Our Father is not seeking to merely civilize us; He wants us to become Christlike. He desires that our confidence in life would be drawn from His union with us.

For most of us, however, our sense of security is rooted in the familiar. How difficult it is to grow spiritually if our security is based upon the stability of outward things! Our peace must come from God, not circumstances, or even relationships. Our sense of reality needs to be rooted in Christ. When it is, the other areas of our lives experience God's security.

Yet, our fears run deep and are many. Indeed, most of us pass through life umbilically tied to the boundaries of the familiar. Even negative experiences, because they are familiar to us, have a way of drawing us back into destructive choices and lifestyles. Why is it that people who have been delivered from adversity are often drawn back into the same problems? Perhaps it is because they are more comfortable with a familiar adversity than they are with stepping into the cold world of the unknown. Consider: many who have spent extended time in jail will return again simply because they are more accustomed to imprisonment than freedom. The coping skills they develop are more suited for jail than for an open society.

People seem to have a latent fear of leaving the familiar. It is significant that, worldwide, most people live within fifty miles of their birthplaces. Humans are cocooned, insulated against change, by the familiar. When we work all day only to come home, watch television, and then collapse into bed, our lifestyle can become a form of bondage. These things may not necessarily trap us in sin as much as they distract us from God.

Moses would leave what was familiar and pitch his tent "outside the camp," where he then sought the Lord.

> Therefore Jesus also, that He might sanctify the people through His own blood, suffered outside the gate. So, let us go out to Him outside the camp, bearing His reproach. For here we do not have a lasting city, but we are seeking the city which is to come. —Hebrews 13:12-14

In the same way that Moses and "everyone who sought the Lord" went outside the camp, and as Jesus Himself went "outside the camp," so also must we, at times, leave the comfort of what is otherwise predictable and set our hearts after God.

This is one reason why Jesus said, "When you pray, go into your inner room, close your door and pray" (Matt. 6:6). Christ desires us to leave the intoxicating world of our senses and learn to abide in the world of our hearts. It is here that we engage in the highest of life's pursuits: to truly find God.

Every minute we seek God is a minute enriched with new life – new power from above. Give yourself a minimum amount of time (an hour or two each day), but do not set a maximum, as the Lord may draw you to seek Him on into the night. And continue day by day, week by week, until you have drawn near enough to God that you can hear His voice, becoming confident that He is close enough to you to hear your whisper (James 4:8).

Let us begin our journey by seeking more of God. Let us not be limited by the boundaries of familiarity. God has more for us than simply attaining an average life. Let us, therefore, secure our tents in the presence of God.

Master, I confess that, in many ways, I have been held captive to the routine dynamics of my life. Forgive me, Lord. I want my walk with You to be genuine. I want You to live in every area of my life: in my thoughts, in my love, in my dreams and in my deeds. Lord, I am hungry for Your presence. Amen.

Adapted from *Holiness, Truth and the Presence of God*

TWO

EVERYONE WHO SEEKS FINDS

It is not hard to recognize one who has spent extended time at a newsstand: his conversation overflows with the drama of current affairs. And, it is not hard to discern a person who has come from a sporting event, as their face reveals the outcome of the game. Likewise, people can tell when an individual has spent extended time seeking God. An imperturbable calm guards their heart, and their countenance is radiant with light, as with the morning dew of Heaven.

Beloved, to seek and find God is everything.

The Eternal Imprint

It is to our shame that, in our era, church services do not focus more on actually seeking God. Yes, we do honor God and thank Him for what He has done. We hear a sermon and, perhaps, enjoy a time of fellowship with others. Yet only rarely do we depart a congregational meeting with the fire of eternity reflecting off our faces. Instead, we fill up with information about God without actually drawing near to Him. Most of us are still largely unaware of God's presence.

While we rightly need church programs, fellowship, and times for ministry training, we must not automatically assume that religious indoctrination is the same thing as actually seeking God. And while I am often blessed listening to contemporary Christian music, even godly entertainment is no substitute for my own worship encounter with God.

Therefore, let us ask ourselves: Is there a place and a time set apart in our spiritual lives where we can give ourselves to seeking God? What if the Spirit of God actually desired to manifest Himself during our worship service? Would the Lord have to wait until we finished our scheduled program? I respect and recognize the need for order; we need the scheduled times for announcements and the defined purposes that currently occupy Sunday mornings, but have we made room for God Himself?

"He Knew Not That His Face Shone"

When we first determine to draw near to God, it may seem we have little to show for our efforts. Yet, be assured: even the *thought* of seeking God is a step toward our transformation. Still, we often do not notice the first signs of our spiritual renewal, for as we grow increasingly more aware of God, we simultaneously grow increasingly less aware of ourselves. Though we may not see that we are changing, others certainly will.

Consider the experience of Moses. The Lord's servant had ascended Mount Sinai, and there stood before the living God. The eyes of Moses were actually filled with God's sun-like glory; his ears actually heard the audible sound of the Lord's voice. Yet, when Moses returned to the people, the Bible says he "did not know that the skin of his face shone" (Exod. 34:29). When the Israelites saw the fire of God's glory on the face of Moses, "they were afraid to come near him" (v. 30). They saw he had been with God.

The church needs more people who have, like Moses, climbed closer to the Almighty, people who have stood in the sacred fire of God's presence. Instead, we exhaust ourselves arguing over peripheral doctrines or styles of music in our song services. Perhaps there are benefits to constantly debating the nuances of our doctrines, but are we not more truly thirsting for the reality of God?

The Enemy's Resistance

What happens when we seek God? The Bible says at the very moment we are drawing near to Him, the living presence of God Himself is drawing near to us (James 4:8). Help is coming, redemption for our situation is on its way, strength will soon be arriving and the powers of healing activated.

But, one may argue, what if we seek Him and He does not come near. Fear not, He will. He may not manifest as we supposed, but He will come. However, let us also acknowledge there may be a spiritual battle. We must be persistent.

Recall the experience of the prophet Daniel (Dan. 10:2-13). For three weeks he sought the Lord with fasting and mourning. Then, suddenly, an angel of the Lord appeared to him, assuring him that "from the first day that you set your heart … on humbling yourself before your God, your words were heard" (v. 12). What took so long? The "prince of the kingdom of Persia," a demonic spiritual ruler, stood against the angel sent to Daniel. There was spiritual warfare.

So strengthen your heart for the likelihood of battle. There may be delays and resistance. Remember, it is those who overcome who inherit the promises of God.

HUMAN FRAILTY

Beyond the obstacles caused by spiritual warfare, we also have inherent weaknesses that can hinder our quest for God. For example, you begin to seek God, but instead of making progress, you find yourself distracted, thinking of things you need to do. To silence a persistent memory, simply write down the things it tells you. Once they are written down, your memory will quiet and your heart will return to seeking God.

Another hindrance to drawing closer to God may be the emotional burdens we carry. Just as we have cleared our memory issues, so we should take time to cast our burdens upon the Lord (1 Pet. 5:6-7). Ironically, our cares and worries may have helped motivate us heavenward, yet they can also dominate our consciousness and, together with other issues, even "choke the word" (Matt. 13:22), leaving us unfruitful in our pursuit of God.

So, as you seek the Lord, as issues and personal concerns arise, place your burdens upon the Lord's shoulders. If your concern is for a loved one, commit that person into the Lord's keeping; if you are struggling with sin, ask God for forgiveness. If it is unresolved conflict with another person, forgive them as much as you presently can, and move closer to God.

If you are troubled by the lack of depth in your forgiveness toward others, remember: the grace to fully release people who have wounded us does not abide with us but in Christ. The closer we draw to Him, the greater power we possess over sin and our reactions to life.

Our goal is to, day by day, draw nearer to God. He has commanded that we come boldly to His throne of grace. To receive the help we need, we must arrive at His throne. Remember also that our confidence comes from Christ Himself. He promised, "Everyone who asks receives, and he who seeks finds, and to him who knocks it will be opened" (Matt. 7:8).

We are seeking a lifetime of increasing devotion, though it may certainly begin in a season of drawing near. In spite of natural and spiritual obstacles, as we persevere, the Lord assures us, "How much more will your Father who is in heaven give what is good to those who ask Him!" (Matt. 7:11).

If we do not cease seeking and knocking, we will discover un-folding degrees of intimacy with God. Even now, He's drawing near. The Lord promises, "Everyone who … seeks finds" (Matt. 7:8).

Master, to possess more of You is the heart-focus of my exis-tence. Draw near, blessed Redeemer, fulfill Your desire for me by fulfilling my desire for You.

THREE

"COME AND SEE"

John and Andrew began their spiritual commitment to God as disciples of John the Baptist. In fact, they had actually been standing near the prophet when Jesus walked by. As the Baptizer saw Jesus, he cried out, "Behold, the Lamb of God!" and from that moment the two disciples began to follow Jesus (John 1:35-37).

This was an insightful account. It is John's handwritten testimony of how he came to the Son of God. Yet, John has deeper truths to reveal beyond this historic portrayal. He is also going to reveal what we should each ultimately seek when we come to Christ.

Let's pick up the narrative. The two disciples, having heard and believed John's messianic proclamation about Jesus, are now walking, perhaps hurriedly, to catch up to Jesus. They are within conversation range.

> Then Jesus turned, and saw them following, and saith unto them, What seek ye? They said unto him, Rabbi, (which is to say, being interpreted, Master,) where dwellest Thou? He saith unto them, Come and see. —John 1:38-39 KJV

There are many reasons one comes to Christ. We may seek Him for health issues or to possess the keys to prosperity. Perhaps we need deliverance or are burdened with the cares of a loved one. Yet, as the Lord asked John and Andrew, so He asks each of us: *What are you seeking in life?* What goals compel us? When we approach the final season of our lives, will the things we have achieved be transferable into eternal accounts? Or will we have spent our time and energies on that which is void of true life?

Jesus asks, "What are you seeking?" It is a very important question. The Lord desires that we take inventory of our passions and objectives, and then chart our course toward heavenly values. You see, many say they love Jesus. What they mean is that, in time, they hope to get around to loving Jesus. Right now, however, they barely know Him and almost never spend time seeking Him.

The proof that we love Him is that we keep His commandments (John 14:15). What must He think when so many who say they love Him are, in fact, not loving Him but actually having an affair with this world? May God have mercy.

Yet, this is not your situation. In spite of your flaws and weaknesses, you sincerely desire to possess more of God. You have emerged from your past trials, determined to walk closer to the Lord. Indeed, Christ sees this holy desire and, to Him, it is the most precious part of you.

The Lord's heart is also moved toward those who follow Him, though they may walk limping. To those wounded by injustice or the effects of sin, the Lord's promise remains faithful: "A bruised reed He will not break and a dimly burning wick He will not extinguish." Surely, He will bring to victory the justice due you (Isa. 42:3; Matt. 12:20).

Like John and Andrew, we, too, "behold the Lamb of God." Just as He asked them, so He turns and asks us, "What are you seeking?"

The Dwelling Place of Christ

In response to Jesus' probing question, the disciples' answer may seem strange. For they did not ask Him for greater power or one of His many spiritual gifts. Instead, they asked Jesus something more personal, and intimate: "Where dwellest Thou?"

I'd like us to consider the poignancy of their answer. They wanted to know where Jesus *lived.* There are times when a question transcends the simple boundaries of intellectual curiosity and actually reveals one's quest in life. Such is now the case: they are seeking to *live* with Jesus. They are searching for the dwelling place of God.

Our Father wants us to ask for spiritual gifts and special blessings of health and financial prosperity. To desire these things is not wrong; it is just not enough. Inside the heart of a God-seeker is a quest for more. We are in search of the "dwelling places" of God. In truth, our hearts have been divinely programmed. There are within us "the highways to Zion" (Ps. 84).

Our destination is nothing less than oneness with Christ. All fruitfulness comes from living in spiritual union with Jesus. In contrast, whatever we offer as service to God that is not the result of our union with Christ, that labor is in vain; it is a weak comfort. For apart from Him, we can do nothing.

John tells us in his first epistle that those who say they abide in Him ought to walk "in the same manner as He walked" (1 John 2:6). Abiding in Jesus leads to walking like Jesus.

Beloved, there is yet much more to learn and discover concerning our Lord! We must beware of spiritual complacency. Recall the prayer of Moses: At the end of his life – after being used by God to confront and defeat the gods of Egypt, after dwelling in the Lord's glory and beholding miracle after miracle for forty years – Moses prayed, "You have begun to show Your servant Your greatness and Your strong hand" (Deut. 3:24).

You have begun? No matter how much we attain, no matter what revelations of God's glory are ours, we have only begun to see His glory.

The disciples answered astutely, "Rabbi, where dwellest Thou?" May this become our prayer as well: *Where do You live, O Son of God? Where is Your dwelling place?* To all who feel similarly, Christ says to us what He promised them: "Come and see."

Dear Master, I turn to You now. You are my life's greatest goal. I desire to live with You, to abide in the wonder of a life united with You.

FOUR

THE NEARNESS OF
OUR GOD

In the 73rd Psalm, the psalmist Asaph expressed a struggle we all might feel at times. He questioned why the wicked seem to prosper while the righteous are chastened. The whole idea was troublesome until he entered the sanctuary of God. Once in the presence of God, Asaph realized his error. As he compared himself to the unbeliever, he saw that, apart from the influence of God, he had nothing in which to boast. He said, "When my heart was embittered and I was pierced within, then I was senseless and ignorant; I was like a beast before You" (vv. 21-22).

Finally, his soul brightened as he considered that God alone was his salvation, and his relationship with God was his strength. He wrote, "Nevertheless I am continually with You … You will guide me, and afterward receive me to glory. Whom have I in heaven but You? And besides You, I desire nothing on earth … God is the strength of my heart and my portion forever" (vv. 23-26).

The summary thought of Asaph's revelation, and the point of this chapter, is in verse 28. He wrote, "But as for me, the nearness of God is my good."

Let's settle this truth once and for all: *it is the nearness of God that produces our good.* Christianity was never designed by God to be sustained by nice people trying to appear good. We're not that good. We're not that clever. And we're not that nice. The only thing that can sustain true Christianity is true union with Jesus Christ. It is nearness to Him in all things that produces our spiritual fruit.

If we are honest, we will admit that, apart from the influence and work of God, there is nothing morally superior or remarkably virtuous about our lives. Our flesh has the same carnal passions as do people in the world; our soul carries within it the same insecurities and fears. Apart from the influence of Christ in us, there's no difference between Christians and non-Christians (except that Christians, when living separate from God's presence, can be more obnoxious). It's only our relationship with the Lord that keeps us from fulfilling the lusts and desires of the flesh, for apart from Him we can do nothing (John 15:5).

Therefore, the strength of our walk does not originate from within ourselves; rather it comes from our relationship with Christ. Our virtue, if it can be defined as such, is that we have learned to prioritize seeking God; our character is the offspring of our oneness with Jesus. By this I mean, Jesus is not only first on our list of priorities; His influence rules over all our priorities. He inspires love in our relationships; His voice becomes the conviction in our integrity. God has made "Christ Jesus" to be to us "wisdom … and righteousness and sanctification, and redemption" (1 Cor. 1:30).

Thus, the God-seeker desires to find the Lord's pleasure drawn to every aspect of his soul. He also knows that, should an area of his heart exist in isolation from God, he will remain vulnerable to manipulation by the enemy in that area. So let me underscore the psalmist's truth, and let us say with our own voice of conviction: it is the nearness of our God that is our good.

A Seeking Heart

Those who pursue God find the path to the blessed life, and those who possess a seeking heart will ultimately be positioned in the brightness of God's pleasure.

What is the nature of a seeking heart? In its initial stages, it involves starting our day in prayer and the study of God's Word, being faithful to write down and obey what the Lord says (Isa. 50:4-5). Yet, when this private time is over, it does not mean we have stopped seeking God. A man with a seeking heart continues his pursuit of God, even in the activities and decisions made throughout the day.

You see, a God-seeker has been trained inwardly by the Holy Spirit so that his soul leans upon God for everything. The godly man has become perfectly weak, therefore God can show Himself as perfectly strong.

Let me give an example. I have a friend, a businessman, whose work depends greatly upon his "personal digital assistant" (PDA), which is a small, handheld computer (also called a smartphone). My friend carries this device with him everywhere. It reminds him of appointments and provides him with numerous details concerning his personal contacts. His PDA is connected to the Internet so that he has access to unlimited realms of knowledge. Finally, it comes with global positioning capabilities (GPS), so that he is always informed of road conditions and traffic; even when he travels somewhere unfamiliar, he never gets lost. My friend has developed an intellectual dependency upon his PDA.

In a similar, yet far more transcendent way, we too must develop a consciousness that depends upon the nearness of God. He organizes, directs and informs us in life so that, even if we are traveling somewhere unfamiliar, we never get lost. As my friend developed a learned dependency upon his PDA, so the Holy Spirit must break us of our independence; we must learn dependency upon God in all things. We must be conditioned to be aware that the Lord is with us, and when we cannot sense His nearness, we should feel troubled and vulnerable until we find Him again.

THE CHRIST PATTERN

The seeking heart habitually looks to God. Was not this the inner working of Christ's heart? Yes, consider the perfections of Christ. Though He was the embodiment of God in Heaven,

He laid aside His privileges of equality with God. Instead, He "emptied Himself" taking the appearance of a man, and as such patterned for us the way of a perfect man with God (Phil. 2:6-8). What we see in Christ is, in truth, not merely the perfection of one's talent or leadership abilities; in Christ we see the perfection of a surrendered heart. Jesus lived a sinless life, yet His power was not inherent, but that which grew out of His deep dependency upon the Father. Christ's incomparable righteousness, His stunning virtue and unparalleled character all had to be appropriated daily as He sought the Father.

Christ shows us how God, manifested as a Son, submits to God the Father. In so doing, Jesus also reveals how man, made in the image of the Son, likewise must draw his spiritual substance from God as his source.

It staggers me that the Son of God said of Himself, "Why do you call Me good? No one is good except God alone" (Mark 10:18). Of course Jesus was good! He was perfect. He who gazed upon Christ, feasted upon God. Yet, even here, Jesus models the pattern we must follow if we would find true spiritual fulfillment.

Christian, let us grasp this one great truth: *attaining righteousness is the result of seeking God*. Jesus had no plan of action other than to mirror the things He saw His Father doing. Everything we see Jesus accomplish on earth was, in fact, the result of His times of seeking God. We see the boldness of Christ and assume He moved in great faith and authority – and He most certainly did. Jesus was bold, but He was never self-willed. His faith came from seeing and hearing the Father. Whether by intuition or by physical sight or by hearing God's voice, Jesus had an inner "radar" that kept Him continually tracking and following the Father's heart.

Jesus did nothing on His own initiative (John 5:30; 8:28). The pattern He set for us is not one of a man wielding unlimited power, but a man pure in heart, seeking God as both a Son and servant. In so doing, He perfectly demonstrates that, when we ask for power or virtue from God, we are, in fact, asking to be nearer still to God the Father. The pure in heart see God; the work of power is, in truth, an act of obedience to what God revealed beforehand.

Do Not Seek Signs, Seek God

The power to work miracles does not come from a secret ministry technique but from the overflow of time spent seeking God. Jesus heard from God. He knew which sick person the Father would heal on which day, and in what manner the healing would come. He also knew who would *not* be healed. He could confidently walk past perhaps dozens of sick bodies at the pool of Siloam and arrive at the one individual God intended to heal.

All that Jesus accomplished was drawn from seeking and finding the Father, and repeating what He saw the Father doing. Some of us, on the other hand, can seemingly go days without drawing near to the Lord. If Jesus Himself could not sustain His heart apart from His relationship with the Father, why do we think we can?

Jesus can produce tremendous fruit in our lives, but only if we learn to become those who seek hard after Him. Our goal is to abide in Him. To abide in Him means we live in a moment-by-moment surrender to Christ. We look to Him; He supplies power and virtue to us. We depend upon Him, trusting and living in the reality of His Word, filled and flush with the life of His Spirit.

We are branches on the vine of God. We are a new species of man, a creature whose life comes not only from the natural world but also from our dependency upon God. May our hearts cease looking for help elsewhere, for it is the nearness of our God which is our good.

Lord, I thank You for this message. I realize You love me and desire my love, and that this word is an expression of Your love for me. Forgive me for living detached from You. I set my heart to live in Your presence. In Jesus' name. Amen.

FIVE

The Earth Is Full of God's Glory

There are many legitimate reasons to seek God, and the Lord graciously receives them all. Yet, it is only because we do not truly know Him that our motivation is primarily crisis-driven. Let us, therefore, boldly bring our needs to Him, but let us also lift our eyes higher and behold the One who helps us. For if we will truly seek the Lord's glory, we will discover, in hindsight, that all our needs are met as well.

Light Shines in the Darkness

It is not enough to know God exists. If we will live in the awareness of the heavenly, we must be freed from the boundaries of the earthly. To awaken faith, the Holy Spirit will take us through times when the presence of God cannot be clearly discerned. The Lord's goal during these times is to bring to maturity our spiritual senses.

Therefore, do not accept that God has permanently hidden Himself from you, though during trials it may seem so. He is teaching us to see in the dark and to hear in the silence. He is making Himself known to our inner man so that, regardless of outer circumstances, we can continually be led by His Spirit.

To see God, beloved, it is imperative that our vision become spiritual and not just sensory. To hear God, we must learn to tune out the clamor of our fears and earthly desires. The outcome of this inner spiritual working is an increasing perception that nothing is impossible for God. The time of darkness, though it comes as an enemy, actually compels us to seek God more earnestly; we learn to even more revere God's light. Never mistake temporary darkness for permanent blindness, for today's training is the very process that opens us to see God's glory. Ultimately, we will discover the truth of what Isaiah wrote, that "the whole earth is full of [God's] glory" (Isa. 6:3).

LORD, OPEN OUR EYES!

Did not Moses endure "as seeing him who is invisible" (Heb. 11:27 KJV)? Indeed, the Bible was written by individuals who actually beheld the glory of God. To see the glory of God is our call as well. Our spiritual vision is not an imaginary device of the mind, but that which comes from the living union of the Holy Spirit with our hearts. Did not our Lord promise that the "pure in heart ... shall see God" (Matt. 5:8)? And is it not reasonable to expect that, if Christ truly dwells within us, we ought to perceive life with unveiled minds? Just as it is written,

> But we all, with unveiled face, beholding as in a mirror the glory of the Lord, are being transformed into the same image from glory to glory, just as from the Lord, the Spirit."
>
> —2 Corinthians 3:18

Yes, if we remove the veils of sin, shame and self-absorption, if we persist in seeking God, staying focused upon His Spirit and Word, we should expect to see the glory of the Lord. Such open perception is biblical and should be pursued! Yet there are those who say access to greater spiritual realities is a false hope and a heresy. I say, beware of the leaven of these unbelieving Christians. For such people would have you accept religion without vision as though to see God's glory was sin.

Consider how many in the Bible actually saw the glory of the Lord: Abraham saw the Christ's glory while he was in Mesopotamia. Isaiah beheld Him in the year King Uzziah died. Ezekiel fell before the Living One by the river Chebar. David, Habakkuk, Solomon, and Zechariah all saw the glory of the Lord (Acts 7:2; Isa. 6:1; Ezek. 3:23; 2 Sam. 6:2; Hab. 3:3; 2 Chron. 7:1; Zech. 1:8).

Moses beheld Him, then Aaron, Nadab, Abihu, and the seventy Hebrew elders as well. Exodus tells us these men actually "saw the God of Israel." The Bible describes this incredible scene, saying that "under [God's] feet there appeared to be a pavement of sapphire, as clear as the sky itself" (Exod. 24:10). The concluding thought is staggering; it reads, "And they saw God, and they ate and drank" (Exod. 24:11).

Think of it: *they beheld God!* Could anything be more wonderful? Is there not a jealousy within you for that experience – *to actually gaze upon the God of Israel?*

Be assured, to behold the Lord's glory is not only scriptural but *typical*, especially during the pivotal decades between ages (which is where we are today). The fact is, over six million Israelites saw God's glory on Mount Sinai. Young men, old women, and little children – people of every age and physical condition – all saw "the glory of the Lord [as it] rested on Mount Sinai" (Exod. 24:16). These same people actually "heard the voice of God" speaking to them (Deut. 4:33)!

Yet, that unveiling of glory did not stop at Sinai. The entire Hebrew nation followed a cloud of glory by day and was illuminated by a blazing pillar of fire-like glory at night. This happened not just once or twice but every day for forty years! How much more shall the Lord of glory manifest Himself to us at the end of the age?

If you are a God-seeker, except for times of darkness when the Spirit refines your spiritual senses, you should expect to see the glory of God! There should be an anticipation that, any day now – as you enter your prayer room or go for a walk, or in a dream

– the Spirit of God is going to appear to you in some marvelous and life-changing way.

I Was Always Beholding the Lord

David wrote a profound statement. He said, "I saw the Lord always in my presence" (Acts 2:25). Something within him, a spiritual radar, caused David to perceive the Lord inwardly, and it caused him to perceive the Lord outwardly. At another time, perhaps while he was watching a sunset with the huge rays of light exploding from behind clouds, David had a revelation: The sky wasn't just a canopy covering the earth. It was, in fact, a declaration of the very glory of God (Ps. 19:1).

I am stunned each time I pause and then lift my eyes and heart upward toward a cloudless night sky. Surrounding us are billions of galaxies, with trillions of stars, all designed and created by our God. He is utterly amazing!

The earth, the surrounding skies – the very mystery and miracle of life itself – all bear witness to a Creator so unlimited in His abilities that men, regardless of their cultural or religious background, have no excuse to not honor Him. Our world is a kaleidoscope of wonders and divinely engineered realities, fitly joined together to showcase the greatness of God.

Recall also Paul's words, that the invisible attributes of God – His eternal power and divine nature – are "clearly seen, being understood through what has been made" (Rom. 1:20).

So, let me ask again: *Have you seen today the glory of God?*

JESUS AND NATURE

Finally, our Lord loves creation. Let us incorporate into our understanding of what it means to become Christlike the fact that, clearly, Jesus loved the created world around Him. You'll recall that He often spent nights praying, and then sleeping, beneath the stars. For forty days in the wilderness, as night fell He lay gazing upon the bejeweled, celestial sky. Indeed, Jesus frequently drew revelation about the Father from the observable world around Him. He told His disciples to "consider the lilies" (Luke 12:27), and spoke of God's love and care, even for the sparrows (Luke 12:6). He saw miracles of life contained within the power of a simple seed, and He brought this revelation into His teaching about the Word of God, itself being a spiritual seed (Matt. 13).

Indeed, many of the Lord's greatest sermons were presented, not in the temple or behind the pulpit of a local synagogue, but at lakesides or on hilltops. Jesus "often met … with His disciples" in the garden of Gethsemane (John 18:2). I love the fact that the Lord routinely found joy among flowers and the landscaping of Gethsemane's garden, and that He brought His disciples there to teach them.

Recall, as well, that it was in this same garden that Christ found strength from God to go to the cross. Yet not only was a garden a familiar place for Jesus while He was alive, but even in death His tomb was set in the midst of a garden (John 19:41). In fact, when He rose from the dead, a distressed Mary thought Him to be the gardener (John 20:15).

Jesus, obviously, saw the creation as an echo of the Father's heart. He found in nature a place, a quiet place, to seek and find communion with God.

Today, many are wearied from battle and wasted from warfare. Yes, we should find solace in God alone, but may we also seek God in settings surrounded by His creation? A God-seeker carries in his heart an appreciation for the world our Father has given us. Our planet is spectacularly beautiful. In seeking God, remember: He is "clearly seen through what has been made."

So let me ask again, Have you seen God's glory today?

Lord, this day I ask You for eyes that see and ears that hear. I desire to find You in moments of stark encounters with You, and also in the world around me. Master, You taught that the pure in heart would see You. Lord, work purity in my heart and vision in my eyes, that I may behold Your glory.

SIX

For Dreams to Come True

Just because we walk and talk does not mean we are truly awake. Zechariah was not sleeping when an angel roused him "as a man who is awakened from his sleep" (Zech. 4:1). Perhaps we too need to be shaken from our slumber to possess the promises of God! Amazingly, in spite of all the signs, wonders, and warnings announcing that we are truly in the last days, Jesus said there will also be a mysterious drowsiness that we must discern and overcome. Indeed, immediately after highlighting the various evidences of the end (Matt. 24), He compares the church to virgins who "all got drowsy and began to sleep" (Matt. 25:5).

Virgins sleeping at the end of the age? It seems incomprehensible with the coming "wonders in the sky above and signs on the earth below" (Acts 2:19), not to mention the powerful, worldwide herald of the gospel of God's kingdom. Yet this phenomenon of spiritual slumber, of losing our God-seeking hunger, is something we must guard against.

When this slumbering spirit approaches, it first dulls our perception. Soon, our zeal for the things of God diminishes. We still love the Lord, of course, but our vision sits in the back seat as other less important aspects of life set the direction for our lives. Indeed, from the beginning, the voice of Satan has had this lulling effect on mankind. Eve's excuse for disobedience? "The serpent hath caused me to forget" (Gen. 3:13 Young's Literal Translation).

This sense of spiritual forgetfulness, of drowsiness, is the cloud of blindness that we each must discern and overcome. It was in regard to this that the Holy Spirit spoke to my heart through the following dream:

> There was a temple standing in an open field. My view of the temple was from its side, about 200 yards away. I could not see its front, yet it must have been completely open because great light flashed out from the inside; it pulsed like lightning yet was solid like sunlight. The block of light coursed straight out, and I knew this light was the glory of God.

The temple was so close, just across the field, that I knew with just a little effort I could enter the glory of God. His holy presence was clearly within my reach. There were others also in the dream who were directly in front of me, people I recognized from church. Each one seemed busy. And while the temple and its light were visible and readily accessible to all, every head was bent downward and turned away from the light; each was occupied with other things.

I heard one person say, "I have to do laundry." Another said, "I have to go to work." I could see people reading newspapers, watching televisions, and eating. I was sure everyone could see the light if they wanted to – even more sure that we all knew His glory was near.

There were even a few people reading the Bible and praying, but everyone maintained the downward thrust of their gaze; each had a mental barrier of some kind between themself and the place of God's presence. No one, in fact, seemed capable of standing up, turning, and steadfastly walking into the very near glory of God.

As I watched, suddenly my wife lifted her head and beheld the temple in the field. She stood and walked without pausing toward the open front. As she drew closer to the light, a garment of glory formed and thickened around her; the closer she went, the more dense the light surrounding her became. Finally, she stepped in front of the temple, turned, and stood in full view of the blazing glory of God. Then she entered the temple.

Oh! How jealous I felt. My wife had entered the glory of God before me! At the same time I realized that there was

nothing stopping me from approaching God's presence –
nothing except the multitude of things to do and responsibilities that, in truth, ruled my life more than the voice of God.

Pushing the weight of these pressures from me, I determined
to rise and enter the temple myself.

But, to my great regret, in my dream as I rose up, I suddenly
woke up! The longing and disappointment within me seemed
unbearable. I had been so close to entering God's presence. How
I wanted to enter the temple and be swallowed up in His glory!

I cried, "Lord, why did You let me wake up?"

Immediately, the word of the Lord responded. He said, "I will
not have My servant's life fulfilled by a dream. If you want your
dream to come true, you have to wake up."

Breaking Passivity; Setting Priorities

Beloved, today God is awakening us to the reality of His
presence. The promises the Lord gives us in the Scriptures must
become more to us than dream-like realities reserved only for
the hereafter. Moses frequented the glory of God. Israel's seventy
elders ate and drank in God's resplendent glory (Exod. 24:9-11).
Jesus unveiled God's glory to His key disciples on the Mount of
Transfiguration! Paul says that beholding the glory of the Lord is
the very means of our transformation (2 Cor. 3:18).

For this reason the Scripture says, "Awake, sleeper, and arise
from the dead, and Christ will shine on you" (Eph. 5:14). If we
truly want Christ to "shine" upon us, we must arise from the distractions that entomb us in lethargy and spiritual drowsiness.

Right at this moment, the presence of the living God is near enough to hear the whisper of our hearts. But if we want our dream of standing in the presence of God to come true, we must wake up.

Awaken my heart, Lord. Open my eyes to all that You are and everything we can be together. Lead me to Your presence and show me how to truly keep You first in my life. Show me what will have lasting significance. I want all of You, and I want to experience Your glory!

Adapted from *The Days of His Presence*

SEVEN

FIND GOD!

There is only one thing that keeps most churches from prospering spiritually: they have yet to find God. "How can you believe," Jesus challenged the Pharisees, "when you receive glory from one another and you do not seek the glory that is from the one and only God?" (John 5:44). If we are displaying our spirituality to impress men — seeking honor from others and living to appear righteous or special or "anointed" before people – can we honestly say we have been walking near to the living God? We know we are relating correctly to God when our hunger for His glory causes us to forsake the praise of men.

SEEKING THE GLORY OF GOD

Does not all glory fade in the light of His glory? Even as Jesus challenged the genuineness of the Pharisees' faith, so He challenges us: How can you believe, when you receive glory from one another?

What a weak comfort is the praise of men. Upon such a storm-tossed sea do we seek contentment. Consider: within but a few days after the Lycaonians attempted to worship Paul, they were congratulating themselves for having stoned him! (See Acts 14:11-19.) Consider: Was it not the same city whose songs and praise welcomed Jesus as "King ... gentle, and mounted on a donkey" (Matt. 21:5), that roared, "Crucify Him!" (Luke 23:21) less than one week later? To seek the praise of men is to be tossed upon such a sea of instability!

We must ask ourselves, whose glory do we seek in life, God's or our own? Jesus said, "He who speaks from himself seeks his own glory" (John 7:18). When we speak from ourselves and of ourselves, are we not seeking to solicit from men the praise that belongs only to God? To seek our glory is to fall headlong into vanity and deception. "But," Jesus continued, "He who is seeking the glory of the One who sent Him, He is true and there is no unrighteousness in Him."

The same quality of heart that made Christ's intentions true must become our standard as well. For only to the degree that we are seeking the glory of God are our motivations true! Only to the degree that we abide in the glory of Him who sends us is there no unrighteousness in our hearts!

Therefore, let us give ourselves to seeking the glory of God, and let us do so until we find Him. As we behold the nature of Christ, as our eyes see Him, like Job we "abhor" ourselves and "repent in dust and ashes" (Job 42:6 KJV). As we are bathed in His glory, we shall be washed from seeking the glory of man.

When we truly find Him, no one will have to tell us to be humble. No one need convince us our old natures are as filthy rags. As we truly find God, the things which are so highly esteemed among men will become detestable in our sight (Luke 16:15).

What could be more important than finding God? Take a day, a week or a month and do nothing but seek Him, persisting until you find Him. He has promised, "You will seek Me and find Me when you search for Me with all your heart" (Jer. 29:13). Find God, and once you have Him, determine to live the rest of your life in pursuit of His glory. As you touch Him, something will come alive in you – something eternal, someone Almighty! Instead of looking down on people, you will seek to lift them up. You will dwell in the presence of God. And you will be holy, for He is holy.

My God, forgive me for having squandered so much time, so much of my life, on superficial and meaningless pursuits. You are all. You are my eternity. Set my heart on fire for You; let me burn inwardly for You with a fire only You can satisfy.

Adapted from *Holiness, Truth and the Presence of God*

PART TWO

Created for Intimacy with Christ

Sow with a view to righteousness,
Reap in accordance with kindness;
Break up your fallow ground,
For it is time to seek the Lord
Until He comes to rain righteousness on you.

—Hosea 10:12—

EIGHT

Two Things, Two Things Only

There are so many things to occupy our minds: so many books, so many good teachings that deserve our attention, that say, "Here is a truth." But, as I have served the Lord these past years, He has led me to seek for two things and two things only: to know the heart of God in Christ and to know my own heart in Christ's light.

KNOWING THE HEART OF GOD

I have been seeking God, searching to know Him and the depth of His love for people. I want to know Christ's heart and the compassions that motivate Him, for the Scriptures are plain: Jesus loved people. Mark's gospel tells us that after He taught and healed the multitudes, they became hungry. In His compassion, Christ saw them as "sheep without a shepherd" (Mark 6:34). It was not enough for Him to heal and teach them; He personally cared for each of them. Their physical well-being, even concerning food, was important to Him.

A lad with five loaves and two fish provided enough for Jesus to work a miracle, but this miracle had to come through Christ's willing but bone-weary body. Consider: Christ brought His disciples out to rest, "for there were many people coming and going, and they did not even have time to eat" (Mark 6:31).

Jesus personally had come to pray and be strengthened, for John the Baptist, Jesus' forerunner, had been beheaded earlier that very week at the hands of Herod. It was in the state of being emotionally and physically depleted that Jesus fed the multitudes – not just once or twice but over and over again "He kept giving them to the disciples to set before them" (Mark 6:41).

Thousands of men, women and children all "ate and were satisfied" (v. 42). Oh, the heart of Jesus! The miracle was for them, but we read of no miracle sustaining Him except the marvelous wonder of a holy love that continually lifted His tired hands with more bread and more fish. Out of increasing weakness He repeatedly gave that others might be strengthened!

So, if my quest is to know Him, I must recognize this about Him: Jesus loves people – all people, especially those whom society ignores. Therefore, I must know exactly how far He would travel for men, for that is the same distance He would journey again through me. Indeed, I must know His thoughts concerning illness, poverty, and human suffering. As His servant, I am useless to Him unless I know these things. If I am to actually do His will, I must truly know His heart. Therefore, in all my study and times of prayer, I am seeking for more than just knowledge: I am searching for the heart of God.

KNOWING OUR HEARTS

At the same time, as I draw closer to the heart of God, the very fire of His presence begins a deep purging work within me. In the vastness of His riches, my poverty appears. The psalmist wrote,

> Who may ascend into the hill of the Lord? And who may stand in His holy place? He who has clean hands and a pure heart, who has not lifted up his soul to falsehood, and has not sworn deceitfully. —Psalm 24:3-4

We cannot even find the hill of the Lord, much less ascend it, if there is deceit in our hearts. How does one serve in God's holy place if his soul is unclean? *It is only the pure in heart who perceive God.* To ascend toward God is to walk into a furnace of truth where falsehood is extracted from our souls. To abide in the holy place we must dwell in honesty, even when a lie might seem to save us. Each ascending step upon the hill of God is a thrusting of our souls into greater transparency, a more perfect view into the motives of our hearts.

It is this upward call of God which we pursue. Yet, the soul within us is hidden, crouching in fears and darkness, living in a world of untruths and illusions. This is our inner man, the soul God seeks to save. Have you discovered your true self, the inner person whom truth alone can free? Yes, we seek holiness, but true holiness arises from here; it comes as the Spirit of truth unveils the hidden places in our hearts. Indeed, it is *truthfulness* which leads to *holiness*. God, grant us a zeal for truth that we may stand in Your holy place!

Men everywhere presume they know the "truth" but have neither holiness nor power in their lives. Truth must become more than historical doctrines; it must be more than a museum of religious artifacts – mementos from when God once moved. Truth is knowing God's heart as it is revealed in Christ, and it is knowing our own hearts in the light of God's grace.

As members of the human race, we are shrouded in ignorance. Barely do we know our world around us; even less do we know the nature of our own souls. Without realizing it, as we search for God's heart, we are also searching for our own. In truth, it is only in finding Him that we discover our true selves, for we are "in Him" (Acts 17:28).

Yet, throughout that searching process, as I position my heart before the Lord, it is with a sense of trembling that I pray the prayer of King David:

> Search me, O God, and know my heart; try me and know
> my anxious thoughts; and see if there be any hurtful way
> in me, and lead me in the everlasting way.
>   —Psalm 139:23-24

Let us take a look at the reality of our hearts. I know God has created us eternally complete and perfect in Christ. I believe that. But in the first three chapters of John's Revelation, Jesus did not tell the churches they were "perfect in His eyes." No! He revealed to them their true conditions; He told them their sins. Without compromise, He placed on them the demand to be overcomers, each in its own unique and difficult circumstance.

Like those in the early church, we must know our need. And like them, the souls we want saved dwell here in a world system structured by lies, illusions, and rampant corruption. Our old natures are like well-worn shoes into which we relax; we can be in the flesh instantly without even realizing it. The enemies that defeat us are hidden and latent within us! *Thus, the Holy Spirit must expose our foes before we can conquer them.*

Concerning man's nature, we are told, "The heart is more deceitful than all else, and is desperately sick; Who can understand it?" (Jer. 17:9). Quoting David again, a similar cry is heard:

> Who can discern his errors? Acquit me of hidden faults. Also keep back Your servant from presumptuous sins; let them not rule over me; then I shall be blameless, and I shall be acquitted of great transgression.
>
> —Psalm 19:12-13

There may be errors inside of us that are actually ruling us without our awareness. Do we realize, for instance, how many of our actions are manipulated purely by vanity or the desire to be accepted by others? Are we aware of the fears and apprehensions that unconsciously influence so many of our decisions? We may have serious flaws inside yet still be either too proud or too insecure to admit we need help.

Concerning ourselves, we think so highly of that which we know so little!

Even outwardly, though we know our camera pose, do we know how we appear when we are laughing or crying, eating or sleeping, talking or angry? The fact is, most of us are ignorant of how we appear outwardly to others, much less inwardly before God! Our fallen thinking processes automatically justify our actions and rationalize our thoughts. Without the Holy Spirit, we are nearly defenseless against our own innate tendencies toward self-deception.

Therefore, to truly find intimacy with God, we must first renounce falsehood. In the light of God's grace, having been justified by faith and washed in the sacrificial blood of Jesus, we need not pretend to be righteous. We need only to become truthful.

No condemnation awaits our honesty of heart – no punishment. We have only to repent and confess our sins to have them forgiven and cleansed; if we will love the truth, we shall be delivered from sin and self-deception. Indeed, we need to know two things and two things only: the heart of God in Christ and our own hearts in Christ's light.

My Lord, how complicated I have made my life, how entangled I've become with so many peripheral things. You are my center; knowing You is eternal life. Search me, O God, and in Your grace allow me to search You and know Your magnificent ways.

Adapted from *Holiness, Truth and the Presence of God*

NINE

STANDING BEHIND OUR WALL

The sense of distance we often feel between Christ and ourselves is an illusion. As we enter the days prior to Christ's Second Coming, the Lord shall begin to remove that falsehood. Indeed, He promises, "In that day you will know that I am in My Father, and you in Me, and I in you" (John 14:20).

The Scriptures tell us that Christ is the vine, we are the branches; He is the head, we are His body; He is the Lord and we are His temple. From start to finish, the Bible declares the Lord not only has a dwelling in Heaven, but that He also abides perpetually in redemptive union with His people. The ever-present focus of His activity is to guide us into oneness with Himself.

Thus, for all that the Holy Spirit has come to establish in our lives, whether through gifts, virtue or power, His highest purpose is to lead us into the presence of Jesus. The Holy Spirit labors ceaselessly to establish intimacy between ourselves and the Lord Jesus. Someone once said that *intimacy* means "into-me-see." *Intimacy* means secrets shared. The Father sees us in secret; He establishes within us the "secret place of [His] presence" (Ps. 31:20), where those who fear Him can always find Him (Ps. 27:5).

This union with Christ lifts us higher to a personal, rather than merely academic, relationship with God's Word. We hear the Shepherd's voice speaking to our spirits, bringing comfort, correction and direction (John 10:27). Not only are we privileged to know Christ's teachings, but as we grow, we also discern the tone of His voice in His instruction. This is heart-to-heart intimacy.

Listen to His wonderful promise:

"I am the good shepherd, and I know My own and My own know Me, even as the Father knows Me and I know the Father; and I lay down My life for the sheep."

—John 10:14-15

Jesus says, "I know My own and My own know Me." How intimate is this relationship? Scripturally, the union between Christ and our hearts is of the same quality as His union with the Father. He says it is "even as the Father knows Me and I know the Father."

Finding Our Beloved

Yet, the sense of distance between Jesus Christ and ourselves persists. You may have prayed, *Lord, You said You are with us forever but I feel isolated from You.* If Christ is within us, how can we find the living flame of His presence?

In the Song of Solomon, this quest to find the secret place of His presence is given wonderful expression. The bride says, "Listen! My beloved! Behold, he is coming, climbing on the mountains, leaping on the hills! My beloved is like a gazelle or a young stag" (Song of Sol. 2:8-9).

This is our Lord, full of vitality! He is "climbing on the mountains, leaping on the hills." To see Him on mountains, though, is to behold Him from afar. He remains distant. How do we live in a moment-by-moment sense of His indwelling presence? We still ask, "Where are You, Lord, *within me?*"

The bride continues,

> "Behold, he is standing behind our wall, he is looking through the windows, he is peering through the lattice."
> —Song of Solomon 2:9

Yes, Christ dwells within us, but He is standing behind our walls. Indeed, there are many "walls" between us and the Savior, and all of them are consequences of unrenewed minds and hardened hearts. We have barricaded ourselves behind fears and carnal attitudes; we are held hostage by sin and worldly distractions.

Yet these barriers can be eliminated. To the degree they are removed, we possess *functional* oneness with Christ; we experience true spiritual advancement.

REMOVING THE WALLS

Even now, let us pursue the removal of these barriers.

Imagine that, even as you are reading, the Lord Himself has quietly entered a nearby room. You look, and suddenly the room is vibrant and alive; it is pulsing with waves of light. Instantly, your spiritual senses are flooded with fear and the awareness of God's holiness; living, probing light actually enters you and descends into your heart, illuminating the true condition of your soul. My question: Knowing that Jesus Christ is in the room, would you enter?

If you could not bring yourself to move toward the room, what would be your reason? If it is because you feel you have failed the Lord too many times, then shame has become a "wall" between you and Christ. If fear keeps you distant, then fear is the barrier between God and you; if an unrepentant heart is keeping you from intimacy with Christ, then heart hardness is your cause of isolation.

Remember, the pure in heart see God (Matt. 5:8). If we repent of our wrong attitudes and sins; if, instead of shame and fear, we clothe ourselves with the garments of praise and salvation, the barriers between ourselves and the Lord shall be removed (Ps. 34:3-5).

But let me ask you a second question: *How* would you enter Christ's presence?

It is my opinion that we would not pick up tambourines and dance into His glory. No. When the greatest apostles and prophets beheld Him, His presence caused each to fall face down as a dead man. For me, it would be with great trembling that I would approach the room of His presence. I would inch my way closer.

How can we remove the sense of distance between Christ and ourselves? In the same way we would repent of sin and shame before entering the room, let us turn our gaze toward His living glory. In trembling obedience, let us enter the fire of His presence for, in truth, He is closer than the room next door. He is, even now, standing behind our wall.

Lord Jesus, I remove the wall created by my fears, sin and shame. Master, with all my heart I desire to enter Your glory, to stand in Your presence and love You. Receive me now as I bow before Your glory.

Adapted from *The Days of His Presence*

TEN

UNRELENTING LOVE

The Bible describes our relationship with Christ in strong symbolic pictures of oneness: He is head of a body, husband of a wife, God in His temple. In spite of these and other powerful metaphors, there remains a sense of distance between the presence of the Lord and us. This distance is a removable barrier; in truth, it is a test. Will we persevere in our seeking God until we lay hold of Him and bring His presence back into His church?

THOSE WHO SEEK AFTER GOD

We simply must have more of Jesus. In the face of increasing wickedness in the world, human ideas have fallen short. Those who understand the hour are seeking God. Possessing more of Christ Himself is our only strategy and hope.

Yet, to seek God is to embark on a journey that will include obstacles and spiritual enemies along the way. We must not give ourselves reasons or excuses to fail.

As a pattern, therefore, we will look at the Song of Solomon 3:1-4. Here we find a bride and bridegroom who both are intolerant of the distance between them. The bride in the passage symbolizes the church in her deepest longings for Jesus; the bridegroom represents the Lord.

The bride: "On my bed night after night I sought him whom my soul loves."

On the highest level, seeking God is an action born of love. It is not a matter only of discipline, it is first an awakening of desire. It is not a question of sacrifice but of the passions stirred by unrelenting love. The bride's ability to sleep is gone because her beloved is gone. She must seek him, for such is the nature of love.

Some will say, "But I already know the Lord. I have found Him." In reality, it was He who found us. Our salvation rests securely upon this truth. But while many rest upon Christ having found them, they have little interest in possessing a greater relationship with Him, nor do they realize His desire for us. The bride loves because Christ first loved her (1 John 4:19). She arises now to find Him. In the very love that He inspired, she pursues her beloved.

The apostle Paul wrote, "As many as are perfect, have this attitude" (Phil. 3:15). To seek and know Christ is the attitude of the mature; it is the singular obsession of Christ's bride.

In this maturing process, there will come a point when your love for God will take ascendancy over mere intellectual or doctrinal understanding. The bride of Christ cannot contain her longing or patronize her aching heart; she cannot simply adjust to feeling empty. There is simply no reconciling the passion of her soul with the absence of her beloved.

Note also that there is an unfolding dimension to seeking the Lord. Genuine love for God is an ever increasing hunger. As one would die without food, so we feel we will die without Him. The bride says, "*Night after night* I sought him." She has come to love the Lord with all her heart, with all her soul and with all her mind (Matt. 22:37). Her love has become all-consuming; to accept his absence is impossible.

Overcoming Resistance

Note: the Lord will allow obstacles and delays to deepen and test the character of our love. Thus, the bride acknowledges, "I sought him whom my soul loves. I sought him but did not find him."

Her first attempts at seeking her beloved proved fruitless, yet she does not terminate her quest. Augustine said it well: "God is not on the surface." There is indeed a "secret place of the Most High." Although hidden, it can be found and accessed.

One common deterrent, ironically, is the benevolent effect that comes with drawing nearer to the Lord. Inevitably, the blessings of an answered prayer or a new understanding of Scripture will greet us on our way to God, but we must guard against these signposts becoming our final destination. We must not be content with edification or comfort, only encouraged.

Let us also understand, we will not find His fullness by seeking Him merely in convenient times and comfortable places. Rather, our quest is a determined and continual pilgrimage. It will not end until He is disclosed to us (Phil. 3:12). We are confident, though, for He has promised that in the day we seek Him with our whole heart, we shall find Him (Jer. 29:13). He assures us, "And I will be found by you" (v. 14).

CHRIST OUR LIFE

The bride continues, "I must arise now and go about the city; in the streets and in the squares I must seek him whom my soul loves."

This inexorable woman has risen from the security of her own bed. She has left the comfort of her warm house and now is seeking her beloved in the streets and in the squares. Pastors, be aware: Not all who wander from church to church are uncommitted or superficial Christians. A significant number are honestly searching for Christ. They are asking, "Have you seen Him?"

Not only is the bride in the streets and squares of Christianity; she is facing the force and the power of darkness as well. Yet nothing stops her — not her own need of sleep or her fear of the night. The love of Christ compels her.

However, again she is disappointed: "I sought him but did not find him."

We might think that after so great an effort — and in the face of the seeming reluctance of Heaven to answer her cry — she would feel justified to return home. But she does not. We too must guard against becoming satisfied with our opinion of ourselves: "We prayed; we waited; we searched for God. We did more than other men." This false reward fills the soul with self-exaltation. If we truly want to find Him, we must stay empty and hungry for God alone.

"The watchmen who make the rounds in the city found me, and I said, 'Have you seen him whom my soul loves?'"

From her bed, to the streets, and now to the watchmen, the bride is seeking her lover. Notice that "the watchmen" found her. The watchmen are the modern-day prophetic ministries. Their highest calling is to find the searching bride and direct her to Jesus. While many may come to the seers for a word of encouragement or revelation, the bride is looking for Jesus. Her singleness of purpose is undistracted; she asks the watchmen, "Have you seen Him?"

"Scarcely had I left them when I found him whom my soul loves." This is the greatest motivation for seeking the Lord: *the time will come when you find Him!* You will pass your tests and overcome the obstacles; you will be secure in the embrace of Christ.

She says, "I held on to him and would not let him go."

I am reminded of Mary at the empty tomb of Christ (John 20:11-18). The apostles came, looked in the cave, and went away astounded. But Mary lingered, weeping. The death of Christ was horrible, but the empty tomb was unbearable. She had to find Him whom her soul loved!

The Scripture says that Jesus Himself came to her, but in her sorrow she did not recognize Him. He said, "Woman, why are you weeping? Whom are you seeking?" It is interesting that Jesus connected Mary's inconsolable weeping with her seeking. Blinded by her tears, she supposed He was the gardener.

"Sir, if you have carried Him away, tell me where you have laid Him, and I will take Him away" (v. 15).

"Jesus said to her, 'Mary!' She turned and said to Him in Hebrew, 'Rabboni!' (which means, Teacher)" (v. 16).

Immediately Mary burst from her kneeling position to embrace Christ; she held Him so tightly that, like the bride, she too could say, "I held on to him and would not let him go." I see Jesus smiling, and with great love He gently pushed her back, saying, "Stop clinging to Me, for I have not yet ascended to the Father" (v. 17).

This is a most astounding event. It is a marvel, I admit, that is beyond comprehension. In the mysterious process of the Lord's resurrection – during an interlude between the grave and some stage of His ascension – Christ interrupted His triumphant ascent to appear to Mary. Jesus was drawn – no, compelled – toward Mary's weeping!

I am staggered by this event. Jesus demonstrated that love is the highest, most powerful law of His kingdom. It brings His living presence into the hearts of those who seek Him.

You Have Made His Heart Beat Faster

One last thought, and it is a profound reality: Where was the Bridegroom during the time when the bride was searching? Was He aloof, indifferent, sitting detached in Heaven? No, from the beginning, He had been watching, actually longing, for His bride to find Him.

He now speaks:

"You have made my heart beat faster, my sister, my bride;
you have made my heart beat faster with a single glance of
your eyes."   —Song of Solomon 4:9

You are His bride. He is returning from Heaven for you! The
single glance of your eyes toward Him makes His heart beat faster.
Such love is inconceivable. He sees your repentance from sin as
your preparation for Him – His bride making herself ready. He
beholds you kneeling, weeping at your bedside. He shares your
painful longing. He has been watching. And the bridegroom says,
"The glance of your eyes has made my heart beat faster."

The Lord has a promise for His bride. There is coming a fresh
baptism of love that will surpass all our knowledge of Him. We
will know the height and depth, the length and the breadth of His
love. While yet here on earth, we will be filled with His fullness.
(See Eph. 3:18-19 Amplified.)

We have many tasks, even responsibilities, which have come
from Heaven. However, the greatest need of our soul is to be with
Jesus. The areas of sin in our lives exist simply because we have
lived too far from Him. Let us commit our hearts to seeking our
God. Let us find Him whom our soul loves and bring Him back
to the house of the Lord!

*Lord, even now we lift our eyes toward You. Jesus, grace and
truth are realized in You. Grant us grace that the truth of this
message will change our lives and compel us in unrelenting love to
You! In Jesus' name. Amen.*

Adapted from *When the Many Are One*

ELEVEN

THE BAPTISM OF LOVE

It is hard for us in this anxious, fearful age to quiet our souls and dwell on God in our hearts. We can engage ourselves with Bible study or other acts of obedience. In varying degrees we know how to witness, exhort and bless. We know how to analyze these things and even perfect them. But to lift our thoughts above this physical world and consciously focus on God Himself seems beyond our reach.

To Dwell Upon God

To actually align ourselves with the thoughts of God – knowing Him and experiencing His life – is to enter a place of spiritual peace and emotional protection. It is to receive into our spirits the shelter of God's living presence.

We cannot content ourselves merely with the tasks we are called to perform. Ultimately, we will discover that study and church attendance are but forms that have little satisfaction in and of themselves. These activities must become what the Lord has ordained them to be: *means through which we seek and find God*. Our pleasure will be found not in the mechanics of spiritual disciplines, but only as these disciplines bring us closer to God.

Paul's cry was "that I may know Him" (Phil. 3:10). It was this desire to know Jesus that produced Paul's knowledge of salvation, church order, evangelism and end-time events. Out of his heart's passion to know God came revelation, the writing of Scriptures, and knowledge of the Eternal.

Paul's knowledge was based upon his *experience* with Christ.

On the other hand, we have contented ourselves not with seeking the face of God but with studying the facts of God. We are satisfied with a religion *about* Christ without the reality of Christ.

The Bible is the historical record of man's experiences with the Almighty. Out of the personal encounters that people had with the living God, our theological perspectives have developed. But knowledge about God is only the first step toward entering the presence of God. As much as the Bible is a book of truths, it is also a map to God. As Christians, we study and debate the map yet too often fail to make the journey.

Love Surpasses Knowledge

Paul warned that religious "knowledge," by itself, "makes arrogant," but "love edifies" (1 Cor. 8:1). We need knowledge, of course, but greater still we need to abide in the place of love. Let us organize our knowledge, yet let us find the secret place of God's presence, where our hearts are assimilated into the living substance of Christ's love. This is the shelter of the Most High.

Remember, the apostle's prayer was that we each would "know the love of Christ which surpasses knowledge" (Eph. 3:19). As essential as knowledge is, personally experiencing the love of Christ "surpasses knowledge." Doctrinal knowledge is vital, yet it is love that fills us "to all the fullness of God" (v. 19).

There is a dwelling place of love that God desires us to enter. It is a place where our knowledge of God is filled with the substance of God.

The Amplified Bible's rendering states:

May Christ through your faith [actually] dwell (settle down, abide, make His permanent home) in your hearts! May you be rooted deep in love and founded securely on love, that you may have the power and be strong to apprehend and grasp with all the saints [God's devoted people, the experience of that love] what is the breadth and length and height and depth [of it]; [that you may really come] to know [practically, through experience for yourselves] the love of Christ, which far surpasses mere knowledge [without experience]; that you may be filled [through all your being] unto all the fullness of God [may have the richest measure of the divine Presence, and become a body wholly filled and flooded with God Himself]!

—Ephesians 3:17-19

Is this not our highest passion, "to be rooted deep in love"? What goal could we have that transcends this: to grasp the breadth, length, height and depth of God's love? Is there anything in all the created universe more staggering, or liberating, than to know the love of Christ? Indeed, to be "wholly filled and flooded with God Himself" is the very hope of eternity!

You see, God cannot truly be known without, in some way, also being experienced. If our eyes had never seen a sunrise or a starry night sky, could any description substitute for actually beholding such expansive beauty? Awe comes from seeing and encountering, not merely from knowing intellectually that there is, somewhere, a thing called a sky and that it is beautiful.

Likewise, to truly know God we must seek Him until we pass through the outer, informational realm about God and actually find for ourselves the living presence of the Most High.

This is the "upward call" of God in Christ Jesus. It draws us through our doctrines into the immediacy of the divine presence. The journey leaves us in the place of transcendent surrender, where we listen to His voice and, from listening, ascend higher into His love.

The earth's last great move of God shall be distinguished by an outpouring from Christ of irresistible desire for His people. To those who truly yearn for His appearing, there shall come, in ever-increasing waves, seasons of renewal from the presence of the Lord (Acts 3:19-21). Intimacy with Christ shall be restored to its highest level since the first century.

Many on the outside of this move of God, as well as those touched and healed by it, will look and marvel: *How did these common people obtain such power?* They will see miracles similar to when Jesus Christ walked the earth. Multitudes will be drawn into the valley of decision. For them, the kingdom of God will truly be at hand.

For those whom the Lord has drawn to Himself, however, there will be no mystery as to how He empowered them. Having returned to the simplicity and purity of devotion to Christ, they have received the baptism of love.

Is this possible, my Lord? Is it true that I might know the love of God that surpasses all knowledge? O God, I seek to know You, to live in the substance of Your love. For Your love is the shelter of my protection.

Help me, Master, to recognize Your love, not as a divine emotion, but as Your very substance! Help me to see that it was neither Pilate nor Satan that put You on the cross; it was love alone to which You succumbed. Remind me again that it is Your love that still intercedes for me even now.

Adapted from *The Shelter of the Most High*

TWELVE

BECAUSE HE FIRST LOVED US

D o you love Jesus Christ? Isn't there a part of your heart that not only accepts the truth of Christ's death for you but, in response, actually loves Him for the price He paid? Don't you love His Word, even when it hurts? And don't you appreciate the many times He's rescued you, even from battles caused by your own sin?

For too many people, however, knowing Jesus is superficial; it goes no deeper than agreeing to the historical fact of His existence. Loving Him is a distant, almost unnatural reality for them. Some even take His name in vain or anger.

For *you*, however, the very sound of His name, *Jesus*, calms the troubling in your heart. You often cry at movies that reverentially mention His name. Even if you fall short of your own spiritual aspirations, still you love His righteousness.

The fact that you possess love for Christ, even if your love is imperfect, proves something vital about you. The very existence of your love has been cultivated and awakened by God's love for you. The living Christ has actually approached you. You love Him because He has revealed Himself to you. As it is written, "We love, because He first loved us" (1 John 4:19).

CHRIST, OUR SOURCE OF UNITY

Today, Christians argue about doctrines and divide over perceptions of end-time events. Yet, let us look at the deeper issue: Do we each love Jesus Christ? If so, our love for Him is the result of His love for us. Even if we disagree with one another on minor doctrines we should treat each other with reverence, for Christ has personally loved us.

You see, the proof that we truly know Jesus Christ is not measured by the degrees we post on a wall but by the degree of love for Him that burns in our hearts.

Do you not love Him? Your love is a response to the relentless warmth of God's love for you, and His love has proven itself irresistible. He says, "You did not choose Me, but I chose you" (John 15:16). Again, He says, "No one can come to Me unless the Father who sent Me draws him" (John 6:44). Even our coming to Him is a product of His love for us.

When I say, "I love You, Jesus," it is because at some point long before I knew Him, before I could discern His voice or recognize His influence in my life, a power born of His love was drawing me to Him. Yes, I know I am not worthy, but still Christ loved me. True, I have no righteousness of my own, but I imagine there was a moment in Heaven when the Son turned to the heavenly Father and said, "I love Francis. I will bring him to Myself, show him My ways, and become the strength of his life."

Behold How He Loves Us

Our capacity to actually dwell in Christ's presence is based upon knowing the true nature of God. If we see Him as a loving Father, we will draw near; if He seems to be a harsh judge, we will withdraw. Indeed, everything that defines us is influenced by our perception of God.

If we do not believe God cares about us, we will be overly focused on caring for ourselves. If we feel insignificant or ignored by Him, we will exhaust ourselves seeking significance from others. Once we accept the profound truth that God loves us, that He desires we draw near to Him, a door opens before us into His heart. Here, in the shelter of the Most High, we can find rest and renewed power for our souls.

Our Lord is not distant from us, for He is actually "touched with the feeling of our infirmities" (Heb. 4:15 KJV). He feels the pain of what we experience on earth. He participates in the life we live, for "in Him we live, and move and have our being" (Acts 17:28 KJV). He is not removed from our need; we are His body.

The truth is, we are never alone in our battles. However, if we *believe* we are alone — if we accept the lie that God does not care — our darkened thinking will isolate us from the eternal commitment of our heavenly Father. Beloved, even in our times of sin or rebellion, the heart of God is not far. Consider the Lord's relationship with Israel. Though Israel had sinned and was suffering oppressive consequences, we read that, when the Lord "could bear the misery of Israel no longer," He raised up deliverers (Judg. 10:16; Neh. 9:27). God wasn't distant; He was with them, actually bearing them and their misery!

At Lazarus' tomb, the Bible tells us that Jesus wept. Of course, Jesus knew He was going to raise Lazarus; He knew it six days before He raised Lazarus from death. He wept because those He loved were weeping.

The Spirit of God feels our heartache. He is with us in our conflicts and fears. At the tomb of Lazarus, some suggest that Christ's weeping was actually over the unbelief of His disciples. I think not. When the Lord wept over Lazarus, those who saw Christ saw a man touched by the sorrows of others, and they marveled, "See how He loved him!" (John 11:36).

Our healing comes when we behold how He loves *us*. We are raised from the dead when He comes to the tomb of our spiritual failures and pain (Eph. 2:4-5). He calls us out of death by name.

You see, we must accept the personalization of God's love. He gave His Son for *my* sins, He enlivens His Word for *my* guidance, and His Spirit is with me as *my* helper. If the Almighty is for *me*, who can be against me?

Never wonder if God loves you. Rather, look at your heart. Do you love Him? If so, your love for Him is proof of His love for you. We love because He first loved us.

Dear friend, with wide-eyed wonder, let us behold how He loves us, and be healed of our aloneness.

Heavenly Father, help us to pause, to absorb into our consciousness the impact of Your purposed love for us. Let this wondrous love influence everything we think and all that we do and become: I am my Beloved's and He is mine. Your banner over me is love. Let my life be flavored by Your unfailing mercy until, with all my heart, I love You, even as You have loved me.

THIRTEEN

Love Me Where You're At

I have discovered that, as we seek the Lord, our most difficult periods can be transformed into wonderful breakthroughs into God's love. For me, one such season occurred during the years 1979 to 1981. The association of churches with which I was aligned had fallen under spiritual deception. Not only were its core doctrines increasingly seeded with New Age influences, but immorality crept in, and key leaders began leaving their wives for other women. I could no longer remain silent. As a result, in 1979 I left my congregation in Detroit, Michigan, where I had served as pastor, and traveled to the organization's regional headquarters in Iowa. I came to plead for repentance. However, after meeting with the senior leaders, I was asked to leave the group.

So here we were – we had left our church, we had no money, and we had four little children; we couldn't even afford basic housing. Desperate for anything, we finally found an old farmhouse in rural Washington, Iowa. The home was over a hundred years old, but it actually looked much older. After negotiating with the landlord, we were given a year of free rent provided I did basic repairs to the house, such as cleaning and painting.

Even so, the house needed more than I could provide. The furnace did not work well, so we installed a wood burner stove in the kitchen. That first winter, it turned out, was one of the coldest in Iowa's history. Frost formed on the inside walls, spreading a foot or two around each window; wind chills dropped to 60 below, and even colder on several occasions.

To keep warm each night, the whole family cuddled tightly on one large mattress on the dining room floor, about 18 feet from the wood burner in the kitchen. A fan behind the stove nudged warm air in our direction. My nightly project, of course, was to build enough heat in the stove to keep us warm until morning.

While I worked the fire, I also would pray and seek God. The wood burner became a kind of altar to me, for each night as I prayed, I offered to God my unfulfilled dreams and the pain of my spiritual isolation. Yes, I knew the Lord was aware of our situation.

Though we had virtually nothing, He showed Himself to us in dozens of little ways. I just didn't know what He wanted of me.

As the seasons came and went, another child was born, and then we fostered a young girl from Vietnam, giving us six children. Still, as the family grew, the little area around the wood burner became a hallowed place to me. Even in the summer, I would sit on the chair next to the stove and pray and worship.

I would like to say I found the joy of the Lord during this time, but in truth, though I gradually adjusted to my situation, I felt an abiding misery in my soul. Our deep poverty was an issue (I barely made $6,000 a year), but more than that, I felt like I had missed the Lord. My continual prayer was, "Lord, what do You want of me?"

Three years of seeking God passed, and I still carried an emptiness inside. What was God's will for me? I had started a couple Bible studies and spoken a few times in churches, but I so identified with being a pastor that, until I was engaged again in full-time ministry, I feared I had lost touch with God's call on my life.

In spite of this inner emptiness concerning ministry, I actually was growing spiritually, especially in areas that were previously untilled. I went through the Gospels, hungry to study and obey the words of Christ. Previously, I had unconsciously defined a successful ministry as something born of my performance. During this time, however, the Lord reduced me to simply being a disciple of Jesus Christ.

Indeed, a number of things I thought were biblical I discovered were really just religious traditions. The Lord desired that I take inventory of my heart and examine those few truths for which I would be willing to die. He said the truths for which I would die, for these I should live.

Frankly, things like the timing of the rapture or nuances about worship style or spiritual gifts dropped in their priority, though I still considered them important. Rising to the top of my focus was a passion to be a true follower of Jesus Christ – to obey His teachings and approach life not merely as a critic but more as an encourager. I also found myself increasingly free to enjoy and learn from Christians from other streams and perspectives.

Yet, these changes, though deep and lasting, occurred slowly, almost imperceptibly. They were happening quietly in my heart, and only in hindsight did I see what the Lord had done. Throughout this time, I was preoccupied with feelings of detachment from God's will. My prayer to know the Lord's plan for me continued daily.

THE BREAKTHROUGH

One day, as I stood in the kitchen pantry, I repeated again my abiding prayer: "Lord, what do You want of me?" In a sudden flash of illumination, the Lord answered. Speaking directly to my heart, He said, "Love Me where you're at."

In this time and season, remember, I was not a pastor or minister. I was a television repairman doing odd jobs on the side to provide for my family. I hated what I was doing. In my previous church I taught against TV and now I was "laying hands" on television sets and raising them from the dead! The Lord's answer cut straight to my heart. I was awed at its simplicity! I asked, "Love You where I am at? Lord, is that all You want of me?" To this He responded, "This is all I will ever require of you."

In that eternal moment peace flooded my soul and I was released from the false expectation of ministry-driven service. God was not looking at what I did *for* Him, but who I became *to* Him in love. The issue in His heart was not whether I pastored, but whether I loved Him. To love the Lord in whatever station I found myself – even as a television repairman – this I could do!

A deep and remarkable transformation occurred in me. My identity was no longer in being a pastor but rather in becoming a true lover of God. Having settled my priorities, amazingly, just a couple days later I was invited to pastor a church in Marion, Iowa. In spite of all my previous anxiety about returning to ministry, I did not jump at the opportunity. For I had found what the Lord truly desired of me. Though I eventually accepted this call, my focus was not merely on leading a church but on loving God.

What God Seeks

More than one's ministry, God seeks our love. His great commandment is that we love Him, ultimately, with all our mind, all our heart, and all our soul and strength. If we love Him, we will fulfill all He requires of us (John 14:15). And it is as we love Him that He orchestrates all things to work together for our good (Rom. 8:28).

Beloved, loving God is not hard. We can fulfill any assignment – auto mechanic or housewife, doctor or college student – and still give great pleasure to our heavenly Father. We do not need ministry titles to love the Lord. Indeed, God measures the value of our lives by the depth of our love. This is what He requires of every true God-seeker: to love Him where we are at.

Lord Jesus, the revelation of Your love has swept me off my feet. Lord, You have drawn me and I run after You. Master, even in the mundane things of life, I shall express my love for You. Consume me in Your love.

PART THREE

THE GREAT PURSUIT: CHRISTLIKENESS

Brethren, I do not regard myself
As having laid hold of it yet;
But one thing I do: forgetting what lies behind
And reaching forward to what lies ahead,
I press on toward the goal for the prize
Of the upward call of God in Christ Jesus.

—PHILIPPIANS 3:13-14—

FOURTEEN

I Will Be
Found by You

It is a well-worn verse, frequently quoted and often memorized. Untold millions have found in this promise both direction and comfort. Originally given by the Lord in a dream to King Solomon, it gives us a way back into the favor, and possibilities, of God. Hear, then, the Lord's promise. He said,

"If my people, which are called by my name, shall humble themselves, and pray, and seek my face, and turn from their wicked ways; then will I hear from heaven, and will forgive their sin, and will heal their land."

—2 Chronicles 7:14 KJV

If we will fulfill just four simple yet vital conditions, we can be assured that God Himself will restore to us a blessed life. These four requirements are irreplaceable: He calls us to humble ourselves, pray, possess a heart that seeks His face, and then chart the course of our lives away from evil.

When we discuss seeking God, the Lord Himself has set the priorities. Each condition embodies the essence of what it means to seek and find the living God.

THE STAGES OF SEEKING GOD

The divine pursuit begins with the humbling of self. Until we embrace humility, our natural mind displays itself as a god sitting in the temple of our thought-life. We are ruled by the tyranny of fleshly desires, soulish fears and human ambitions. To advance in God we must retreat from self.

Thus, when true meekness emerges in our hearts, it comes to silence the clamor of our fleshly minds. The volume on our self-righteousness mutes; the voice of our fears and inadequacies becomes a whisper. To humble our earthly perspectives and opinions, we must relegate them to a lower priority; they become mere background noise as our focus turns increasingly toward God. No pretense prevails; we come humbling ourselves. We bow on our face before the holy gaze of God. And in His light finally we perceive the darkness of our soul.

Thus, humility, at its root, starts with honesty. The humbled heart is truly and deeply acquainted with its need and, in the beginning, the awareness of one's need becomes the voice of prayer. This confession, "I have sinned," puts us on the side of God concerning it. We agree with our Father that our behavior is wrong – we're selfish, lustful and unloving. Thus, the process of healing begins during this moment of self-discovery. We are working together with God to defeat sin in our lives, and in this process of humbling ourselves the Lord grants us peace, covering, and transforming grace.

Yet, with humility we not only acknowledge our need, we take full responsibility for it. We offer no defense to God for our fallen condition. We've come, not to explain ourselves but to cleanse ourselves. Though we may have suffered injustice, we abandon self-justification or accusation toward others. We are consumed with the condition of just one soul, our own; and our quest is for mercy, not vengeance.

At some point, however, our humility toward God, if it is genuine, will regenerate and bloom again in our relationships with others. We will be able to laugh at ourselves; we will no longer take offense when challenged or accused. If we have been embittered by life, we now forgive. And, if we sinned against another, we humbly ask their forgiveness. We must deal with our offended heart. The Lord God may not require us to trust everyone, but He does call us to forgive (Matt. 18:21-35).

In a world where the heart of man is "deceitful above all things, and desperately wicked" (Jer. 17:9 KJV), in Heaven's eyes, to tearfully acknowledge our need is a breakthrough.

A People of Prayer

The road to healing a society, whether it is a community, a church, or a family, begins with humbling ourselves to God and to one another. The Lord, who dwells "on a high and holy place," also dwells "with the contrite and lowly of spirit." It is the contrite and lowly the Lord promises to revive (Isa. 57:15).

Yet, humility is not our final goal. We must learn also to be a people of prayer. Prayer is the voice of our dependency. Strong, independent people do not pray; dependent people broken of self-will pray and look to God. Prayer is not a laser beam; it is a prism that accommodates variations of color and expression. Whether our cry is in supplication or silence, regardless if it is tearful or rejoicing, at its core, prayer is not just telling the Lord our needs; it is *transferring* those needs to God.

It should also be acknowledged that, especially in the beginning, prayer is often an expression of fear – fear concerning the threats and conditions of life, and fear that our sin or circumstances will overwhelm us or a loved one. Yet, we do not pray because we fear; we pray because we have a promise from God. He has said He will "hear from heaven … and heal." Thus, at some point, fear must be displaced by faith; our prayer must be an expression of our growing trust in God. The world will remain a fearful place, but prayer empowered by faith can transform our world.

THE GOAL GOD SEEKS

If we humble ourselves and pray, we will have ever increasing access to God. Yet, while we may experience degrees of breakthrough, our hope is to see God actually heal our land. It is encouraging to see that, today, the prayer movement has become a force in the earth.

However, if we are honest, the depth of healing we have sought has not occurred. We have fasted and prayed, but the greatest breakthroughs have not come. Why? *Perhaps we have sought God's hand more than His face.*

First, it is right to seek God's hand. Indeed, Scripture asks, "To whom has the arm of the Lord been revealed?" (Isa. 53:1). Jesus cast out demons by the "finger of God" (Luke 11:20). Seeking the arm or hand or finger of the Almighty certainly is of great value. But the Lord did not say, "Seek My hand." Rather, He calls us to seek His face. We must lift our prayers beyond the needs of our world, and let our highest prayer be to seek God for Himself.

"If My people … seek My face," He says. Until now, our pilgrimage has been about us coming to God with our needs. Now, it is about Him. In this shift of focus, beloved, is the power to turn nations.

When we become true God-seekers – individuals whose delight is perpetually in the Lord – we will secure the full help of Heaven. And more, we will rise to meet the consummate reward of Heaven: to see the face of God (Rev. 22:3-4).

As a leader in the prayer movement, I ask you to join me in making your highest goal to seek the face of God. Whether we live in times of crisis or times of peace, my heart says to the Lord,

"Your face, O Lord, I shall seek" (Ps. 27:8). Yes, we have prayer, and from our hearts we humble ourselves and fast and weep.

In a parallel promise given by God to Jeremiah, the Lord spoke to a people in exile from their land. He assured them that His plan for them was for their welfare and not for calamity (Jer. 29:11). And again He brought their focus to seeking Him. He says,

> "Then you will call upon Me and come and pray to Me, and
> I will listen to you. You will seek Me and find Me when you
> search for Me with all your heart."   —Jeremiah 29:12-13

In the next verse, the Lord reinforces His promise, saying, "And I will be found by you" (v. 14).

The Spirit of God desires not only that we seek Him but that we actually find Him! The humbling of our soul and learning to pray — these are not simply spiritual disciplines or mechanical things we do for the sake of revival. They are heart preparations. The invitation from the Lord to seek His face is not to be taken lightly; indeed, it is staggering!

God desires intimacy with us. To seek His face is to behold the divine expression and to hear the tone of His voice. From the vantage point of His presence, we can truly turn away from evil. For to know His love is to know why we've been created.

God-seeker, do not doubt the outcome of your pursuit. He says with glad assurance, "And I will be found by you."

Oh God, my insides ache for You, to know You and walk in Your ways. You are my exceedingly great reward, the pearl of great price. I love You, Master. And I will seek You until I truly find You.

FIFTEEN

THE RIVER OF GOD'S PLEASURE

To seek the maturity of Christ is to be nourished by the nectar of Heaven. If we will be successful in seeking God, we must not only come with our desire for God, we must also understand His desire for us. On the most fundamental level, God is our Father. His love is unconditional and, in that love, He seeks the best for us.

No true father wants children to grow up rebellious or without knowing their nature and destiny. So in seeking God, we must also ask as a child of God, what does my Father seek from me? The answer to this is the reason for my existence: God seeks to reproduce in us the character, power and love of Jesus Christ, His first-born Son (Rom. 8:29). God heals us so He can transform us to Christ; He forgives us so He can restore us to the path toward Christlikeness. God loves us, yet there is also an eternal purpose working in His love. We are saved so we can "grow up in all aspects into Him who is the head, even Christ" (Eph. 4:15).

What gives our Father His greatest pleasure? Is it not to make man in His image, according to His likeness? (Gen. 1:26-27) *Thus, to fulfill the purpose of God is to fulfill the heart of God.* Each area of our soul that is renewed in the image of Christ is a dimension of our life that exists in functional oneness with our heavenly Father.

Even as we seek God for our needs and intercede for the needs of others, as God-seekers our highest goal is to become Christlike. No doubt we will have times of weakness or even sin; inevitably we will face periods of discouragement and weariness. Yet in spite of setbacks, let us seek to lay hold of the reason God has laid hold of us (Phil. 3:12). If we set God's priority before us, the Lord will meet us on ever transcendent levels.

The Clamor of Many Voices

As the days unfold toward Christ's return, a multitude of voices will clamor for our attention. Additionally, signs and wonders, judgments and upheaval will also burst into the collective consciousness of man, demanding our focus. Our world will experience the increase of sin and lawlessness, which will further deplete the love of many Christians (Matt. 24:12). If we are true seekers of the Most High, we must beware the contagious nature of an embittered heart. We cannot allow ourselves to be infected by, or conformed to, the attitudes of angry, loveless Christians.

These are the "difficult times" (2 Tim. 3:1) Paul warns about. Yes, our world is full of artificially sweetened, salt-free Christians who are trodden underfoot by men. We must not assume it cannot happen to us. Yet, it is in this very environment that our Father has purposed to reveal Christ in us. Even now, our destiny is courting our preparation. Let us press toward full transformation!

CREATED FOR GOD'S PLEASURE

What does it mean to become Christlike? It means we choose to live for one purpose: to give pleasure to God. To accomplish this, we must be intimately acquainted with that in which His soul delights. Jesus always chose to give God pleasure, even in the midst of conflict and cruelty. Thus, when injustice wounds us, we must redeem our experiences with mercy. Let us make the Sermon on the Mount our standard of conduct. Let us discover those ways that will reveal Christ through us and thus bring pleasure to God.

As it is written,

> "Thou art worthy, O Lord, to receive glory and honor and power: for thou hast created all things, and for thy pleasure they are and were created."   —Revelation 4:11 KJV

The key to lasting happiness and true fulfillment in this world is not found in self-gratification but in bringing gratification to the heart of God. And while the Lord desires that we enjoy His many gifts, He wants us to know that we are not only created *by* Him but *for* Him as well.

A "Lay Worker" for God

To His neighbors, Jesus was just a carpenter's son. Yet, to God, Jesus was the one pearl of great price. Indeed, before His public ministry began — before there were any miracles or multitudes — yes, as a carpenter, Jesus' devotion to God flooded the Father's heart with pleasure. At the core of His existence, Christ's motive was always to do only those things that pleased the Father (John 8:29).

It was His desire to please the Father that caused Jesus to perfectly fulfill the Law, and it was to please the Father that He went to the cross. It was not raw zeal for His culture or religion that compelled this carpenter to a sinless life. It was something higher and far more extraordinary: the law of love for God. His passion to give pleasure to the Father was all consuming.

Could Jesus have heard more wondrous words than the praise spoken by the heavenly Father at the Jordan? At the sound of the Father's voice, the heavens opened, the Spirit descended, and the river of God's pleasure flowed outward to His Son. In words unheard by any human being, the Father spoke: "You are My beloved Son, in You I am well-pleased" (Mark 1:11; Luke 3:22).

Remember, Jesus was still a "lay person" during this encounter. He had not yet entered public ministry. I am awed as I consider this reality: *it was Jesus' life as a tradesman, a "blue-collar worker," which increased the Father's bliss!* He did not need miracles and multitudes, or great insights, to touch the Father's heart. He had not yet fasted for forty days. While accomplishing common, everyday tasks, Jesus flooded God's soul with delight!

Likewise, those who truly seek God are dedicated to bringing pleasure to their heavenly Father, even in the common tasks of everyday life. Jesus' ability to please God while working a "secular" job tells us God is seeking something from us that is more hidden, more precious, than the things esteemed outwardly by man.

In other words, God delights in the man or woman who serves Him with joy, even when no one is there to observe or impress. In God's eyes the origin of true ministry is not found in what we do for Him but in what kind of people we become to Him.

No God-seeker Is Insignificant
to the Father

You who seek the Lord ponder this wondrous privilege: *we can bring pleasure to God!* In a world where sin and injustice actually pain the heart of God, with our love and steadfast faith, as we seek God daily, we can please the Father!

To set our goal to reveal Christ is to arouse God's pleasure at its highest level. No one, nor any thing, brings pleasure to the Father as does seeing His Son, even beholding the Spirit of Jesus Christ, revealed in us. Each time we submit to Jesus, giving Him access to this world, we please God. Every time Christ forgives or loves or blesses through us, the heart of God finds pleasure in our lives.

In every one of life's varied and challenging situations, let us seek to know how we may reveal Christ. For in the love between the Father and His Son the river of God's pleasure flows.

Oh God, the thought that my life may bring pleasure to You is so high I can barely believe it. Lord, look upon me as Your workmanship; create in me that which will most glorify You. Make my life an aroma of thanksgiving that ever brings pleasure to Your heart.

Adapted from *The Days of His Presence*

SIXTEEN

THE DIVINE
OBSESSION

There are three basic categories of Christians. The largest group consists of people who, though they try to avoid the darkness in the world, have no hope that the world can be redeemed. Assuming Christ's return is imminent, they retreat into what seems a shelter of apathy concerning the

non-Christian world around them. Yet most are not truly apathetic. Their souls, like Lot's, are vexed by the conduct of unprincipled
men (2 Pet. 2:7-8). Their compassion, though, is kindled even if
it's limited. Rarely do they extend themselves beyond the needs
of their immediate family and closest friends. They love the Lord,
but they don't know how or what to do to change society or even
to positively impact their neighborhoods.

The second group of Christians consists of those who would
rather rail at the darkness than adjust to it. Though much smaller
in number than the first, they are by no means apathetic; in fact,
they appear exactly opposite. They rage at the depravity of the
ungodly and protest the audacity of the wicked. They pound the
pulpit and the pavement; they are both vocal and visible. Yet their
ability to transform their culture is, for the most part, neutralized
by their negativity and rage. They are dismissed as judgmental
extremists. Most sinners simply cannot endure the harshness of
their approach.

Both groups sincerely desire to see our culture transformed. Yet
the same problem afflicts them: they are troubled that the world
is unchristian, without being troubled that their own hearts are
un-Christlike. They do not perceive the priority of God's heart,
which is the transformation of the church into the image of Christ
(Rom. 8:28-29).

WORLD CHANGERS NEEDED

It is this very passion to be conformed to Christ that separates
the third group from the others. Though smallest in number, its
members are the most effective. Throughout history, these have
been the world changers. These are the individuals who have

understood the priority of God. They know that the Father's highest passion is to behold His Son revealed in a believer's soul. As much as they are moved with compassion for the lost, their primary quest is not to touch their neighbors' hearts, but to touch the heart of God. They know if they awaken the Father's pleasure, the power of His Spirit will go before them. God Himself will change the hearts of those around them.

It is my sincere quest in life to be like Jesus in everything. It stuns me to know that if I am truly conformed to Christ, I have the Spirit's promise that I will also awaken the pleasure of Almighty God. Here, in my transformation, is the power to touch cities and redeem cultures, for it takes transformed people to transform nations.

To Be Like Christ

Indeed, it was this hunger for Christlikeness that was the secret of Paul's success. His expressed vision was simply, "That I may know Him and the power of His resurrection and the fellowship of His sufferings, being conformed to His death" (Phil. 3:10).

Paul's passion was taken up with this one heavenly goal: "being conformed" to the life and power of Jesus Christ. The apostle's quest was not only to win the world but to know Jesus Christ. The works Paul accomplished – founding churches, writing almost half the New Testament, winning the lost, demonstrating miraculous spiritual gifts, and remaining faithful throughout times of terrible suffering – were all by-products of his passion to know Christ.

Likewise with us, the Father's immediate, primary goal for the church is for us to be like Christ. He rescues us so He can transform us. Some say that the Father's goal is to win the lost. Yet, if this were His highest priority, He would simply bypass the church and save men Himself.

Has He not proven, as seen in Paul's conversion, that His abilities to save people are without limit? Did He not change the arrogant heart of King Nebuchadnezzar into a man of meekness who gave glory to God? Who can resist Him who is irresistible? However, instead of revealing His glory, it is His choice to reach to the lost through the agency of transformed people.

This, my friends, is the glorious mystery of our existence: the Almighty has purposed from eternity to create a race of men and women who, though tested in a corrupt and violent world, bear the image and likeness of Christ (Gen. 1:27). Christ calls this heavenly-natured people "the church," His "new creation" (2 Cor. 5:17 NKJV).

The Holy Obsession

To be in love is to be obsessed with one's beloved; to be obsessed is "to think continually about the same thing." In this sense, the Father is obsessed with filling the universe with the Spirit of Jesus Christ. Beginning with eternity past, revealing the Firstborn in the womb of time, and continuing with the transformation of the church, the Father desires all creation ultimately to be summed up in Christ. Our goal is to participate in this "summing up" (Eph. 1:10) until all that we are is conformed to Christ.

Now, if the Father is obsessed with His Son, let us also surrender not only to God's will but also to His obsession. Indeed, Jesus prayed that the very love with which the Father loved the Son would be in His disciples (John 17:26). We can receive and be flooded with the very same quality of love that the Father has for His Son. We can know the divine obsession.

Therefore, let us ponder and then pursue what it means to be Christ-like. Let us give ourselves to the divine obsession of God: to see creation, starting with ourselves, summed up in Christ. For it is here, in the transformation of our lives, that we discover and fulfill the wondrous obsession of God: the unveiling of His Son in the earth. It is here, at the threshold of Christ in us, that we discover the power one life surrendered to Christ has upon the heart of God.

Father, let my heart become as obsessed with Your Son as You are. Let the fullness of my absorption with Him displace all other pursuits until, at the mere glimpse of Jesus, my whole being is flooded with the pleasure You Yourself feel.

Adapted from *The Power of One Christlike Life*

SEVENTEEN

TO BEHOLD THE
FACE OF GOD

Have you not deeply desired to see God, to know Him intimately and truly? Beloved, to see Jesus is to behold God. Let us not consider it heresy: *we can surely see God!* But first, we must renounce every perception of the Almighty other than what we have found proven true in Christ.

Therefore, study the life, the teachings and deeds of Jesus Christ, and you will remove the veil of mystery surrounding the nature of God.

Jesus said, "He who has seen Me has seen the Father" (John 14:9).

What truth could be more profound? Each time we read of what Jesus did, we are actually beholding the nature of God. Every time we listen to what Jesus taught, we are hearing the voice of the living God.

Jesus is the image of the invisible Father (Heb. 1:2-3). "In Him all the fullness of Deity dwells in bodily form" (Col. 2:9). Jesus is God's form. He mirrored on earth those things He saw His Father doing in Heaven; He echoed the words the Father whispered to Him from eternity.

Do you truly desire to see God? Christ's words are windows through which the pure in heart behold the Almighty.

Certainly, others can edify our souls greatly, but no prophet, apostle or teacher excels the revelation of God in Christ. Ponder Christ and you contemplate the nature of God. Eat His words and you assimilate into your spirit the substance of the Almighty.

> "God, after He spoke long ago to the fathers in the prophets in many portions and in many ways, in these last days has spoken to us in His Son."   —Hebrews 1:1-2

God spoke to the prophets "in many portions and in many ways." Indeed, all their words inspire, correct and guide our souls; they are all profitable for reproof and correction, that we may be fully instructed. But "in these last days [God] has spoken to us in His Son."

Prophets will point the way; Christ is the way. Teachers will expound the truth; Jesus is the truth. Apostles will proclaim the life; Jesus is the life. Yes, all speak the word, but the Son of God is the Word.

The teachings of Jesus Christ are not to be blended into the Scriptures as though He were one of many equally important voices used by God. He is, in truth, the living revelation of God Himself, the sole expression of His invisible glory. When Christ speaks, we are listening to God unfiltered, unbiased, unveiled.

Blessed Are the Pure in Heart

Jesus said the pure in heart will see God. David wrote, "With the pure You show Yourself pure" (2 Sam. 22:27). Think of it: not only can we truly know God, He desires to show Himself to us. David said, "You show Yourself."

How valuable are Christ's words? To each soul that chooses to abide in the words of Christ, He has promised, "I ... will disclose Myself to him" (John 14:21). His promise is not reserved for a time later in Heaven, but in some deep measure He desires to fulfill His words here, now.

We may have grown content with the illusion of distance; yet God is not content. He created us to live in steadfast union with His presence. The sense of distance between the Almighty and ourselves is a deception.

Indeed, the Lord corrects us not merely because He hates sin but because sin separates us from His presence. He loves us and purifies us so we can see Him.

Remember, beloved, the prayer of Jesus, "Father, I desire that they also, whom You have given Me, be with Me where I am, so that they may see My glory" (John 17:24).

Are we so content with our religion that we ignore this promise? We can be with Him where He is. He is specifically praying that we see His glory.

Abraham, Sarah, Jacob, Joshua, the parents of Samson – Scripture is filled with imperfect people who beheld God's glory and lived to tell about it! Why should you or I be deprived? Jesus said that he who is least in His kingdom is greater than these! The glory which God displayed in the Old Testament, which faded from Moses' face, faded after descending and filling Solomon's temple, departed from Israel during the priesthood of Eli – that glory now dwells permanently in the spirits of those who've been truly born again. The glory in us will not fade but increase, especially as the day of His return approaches! We will be filled with His glory! (2 Cor. 3:7-18)

So, I ask again, would you see God? Would you pursue the glory of the Lord? Study Jesus. Ponder His words and deeds. For to steadfastly gaze upon Jesus is to behold "the glory of God in the face of Christ" (2 Cor. 4:6).

Father, I want to see Your glory and to dwell in Your presence. Answer Your Son's prayer in John 17:24 through me, that I might be with Christ where He is to behold Your glory. Make Your Word come alive to me and let it transform my soul. Renew my mind that I might live in perpetual union with You.

EIGHTEEN

A Place for Him to Rest

In the kingdom, there are no great men of God, just humble men whom God has chosen to use greatly. How do we know when we are humble? When God speaks, we tremble. God is looking for a man who trembles at His word. Such a man will find the Spirit of God resting upon him; he will become a dwelling place for the Almighty.

ENTERING THE SABBATH REST OF GOD

"Heaven is My throne and the earth is My footstool.
Where then is a house you could build for Me? And where
is a place that I may rest?"   —Isaiah 66:1

God asks for nothing but ourselves. Our beautiful church
buildings, our slick professionalism, are nearly useless to God.
He does not want what we have; He wants who we are. He seeks
to create in our hearts a sanctuary for Himself, a place where He
may rest.

In the Scriptures this *rest* is called "a Sabbath rest." It does not,
however, come from keeping the Sabbath, for the Jews kept the
Sabbath, but they never entered God's rest. The book of Hebrews
is plain: Joshua did not give the Israelites rest (Heb. 4:7-8). And
after so long a period of Sabbath-keeping, the Scripture continues,
"There remains a Sabbath rest for the people of God" (Heb. 4:9).
This rest was something beyond keeping the seventh day holy.

The question must be asked then, what is this Sabbath rest?
Let us explore Genesis in pursuit of our answer. "Then God
blessed the seventh day and sanctified it, because in it He rested
from all His work" (Gen. 2:3). Before God rested on the Sabbath,
there was nothing special or holy about the seventh day. Had the
Lord rested on the third day, then it would have been holy. *Rest is
not in the Sabbath; it is in God.* Rest is a prevailing quality of His
completeness.

Revelation 4:6 describes the throne of God as having before it,
as it were, "a sea of glass, like crystal." A sea of glass is a sea without
waves or ripples, a symbol of the imperturbable calm of God. Let
us grasp this point: *the Sabbath was not a source of rest for God; He*

was the Source of rest for the Sabbath. As it is written, "The Creator of the ends of the earth does not become weary or tired" (Isa. 40:28). And even as the Sabbath became holy when God rested upon it, so we become holy as we put away sin and the fullness of God settles and rests upon us.

In our study, we are not associating God's rest merely with the sense of being rebuilt or rejuvenated, which we obviously need and associate with human rest. The rest we seek is not a rejuvenation of our energy; it is the exchange of energy: our life for God's, through which the vessel of our humanity is filled with the Divine Presence and all-sufficiency of Christ Himself.

Enveloped and Permeated with God

The Hebrew word for *rest* is *nuach*; among other things, it means "to rest, remain, be quiet." It also indicates a "complete envelopment and thus permeation," as in the spirit of Elijah "resting" on Elisha, or when wisdom "rests in the heart of one who has understanding" (Prov. 14:33). God is not looking for a place where He can merely cease from His labors with men. He seeks a relationship where He can "completely envelop and thus permeate" every dimension of our lives, where He can tabernacle, remain, and be quiet upon us.

When our hearts have truly entered God's rest, we live in union with Jesus the same way He lived in union with the Father. Christ's thought-life was completely enveloped and thus permeated with the presence of God. He did only those things He saw and heard His Father do. He declared, "The Father abiding in Me does His works" (John 14:10). Likewise there remains a promise of rest for us because it is Christ working through us. Jesus promises us, "If you ask Me anything in My name, I will do it" (John 14:14). How vain we are to think we can perform miracles, love our enemies, or do any of the works of God without Christ doing His works through us!

This is why Jesus said, "Come to Me ... and I will give you rest" (Matt. 11:28). In a storm-tossed boat on the sea of Galilee, Christ's terrified disciples came to Him. Their cries were the cries of men about to die. Jesus rebuked the tempest and immediately the wind and sea became "perfectly calm" (Matt. 8:26), even as calm as He was. What program, what degree of ministerial professionalism can compare with the life and power we receive through Him?

You see, no matter how much we spend of ourselves, our efforts cannot produce the rest or life of God. *We must come to Him.* Many leaders have worked themselves nearly to exhaustion as they seek to serve God. If they spent half their time *with Him,* in prayer and waiting before Him, they would find His supernatural accompaniment working mightily in their efforts. They would become passengers in the vehicle of His will, a vehicle in which He Himself is both Captain and Navigator.

CEASE STRIVING, KNOW, THEN OBEY

To enter God's rest requires we abide in full surrender to His will, in perfect trust of His power. We learn to rest from our works "as God did from His" (Heb. 4:10). It requires diligence, however, to enter God's rest (Heb. 4:11). To rest from our labors does not mean we have stopped working; it means we have stopped the laborious work of the flesh and sin. It means we have entered the eternal works, which He brings forth through us.

The turmoil caused by unbelief is brought to rest by faith. The strife rooted in unforgiveness is removed by love. Our fearful thoughts are arrested through trust in Him; our many questions are answered by His wisdom. Such is the mind that has entered the rest of God.

The church needs to possess the knowledge of God's ways, for herein do we enter His rest (Heb. 3:8-11). We gain such knowledge through obedience to God's Word during conflicts. As we obey God through the testings of life, we learn how to deal with situations as God would. Consequently, it is of the utmost value to hear what God is speaking to us, and especially so when life seems to be a wilderness of hardship and trials.

Therefore, the Spirit says,

"Today if you hear His voice, do not harden your hearts as when they provoked Me, as in the day of trial in the wilderness ... Therefore I was angry with this generation, and said, 'They always go astray in their heart, and they did not know My ways'; as I swore in My wrath, 'They shall not enter My rest.'" —Hebrews 3:7-8, 10-11

He says, "They always go astray in their heart ... they did not know My ways ... they shall not enter My rest." *Knowing God's ways leads to His rest.* We must see that there is no rest in a hardened heart. There is no rest when we rebel against God. Our rest comes from becoming honest about our needs and allowing Christ to change us.

Thus Jesus said, "Learn from Me ... and you will find rest for your souls" (Matt. 11:29). Stop fighting with God and learn from Him. Let the Word of God put to death the torments of the sin nature. Cease struggling and wrestling against the Blessed One.

Trust Him! For eventually His Word will plunder the defenses of your heart. Be committed to the process of surrender. In time He shall no longer use adversity to reach your heart, for you shall delight in being vulnerable to Him. Continue your diligent yielding until even His whisper brings sweet trembling to your soul. Far more precious than the men of a hundred nations is one man perfectly given to the Spirit of God. This man is God's tabernacle, the one to whom God looks and is well pleased. He says,

> "Heaven is My throne, and the earth is My footstool. Where then is a house you could build for Me? And where is a place that I may rest? For My hand made all these things, thus all these things came into being."   —Isaiah 66:1-2

Yet, incredibly, one man with one quality of heart captures the attention and promise of God. "But to this one I will look, to him who is humble and contrite of spirit, and who trembles at My word" (Isa. 66:2).

God looks to the man who trembles when He speaks, whose very core resonates in response to the divine utterance, for in him the holy power of the Most High can abide in perfect peace. He has learned the ways of God; he delights in obedience. He has chosen to give God what He asks: nothing less than all he is. In return, this man becomes a place, a holy place, where God Himself can rest.

Lord, I confess my heart has been too hard. I desire to tremble when I hear You speak. Forgive me for striving, I desire that my spirit would be a place of rest for Your presence. Keep me in Your rest.

Adapted from *Holiness, Truth and the Presence of God*

PART FOUR

Becoming a True Worshiper

"But an hour is coming, and now is,
When the true worshipers will worship the Father
In spirit and truth;
For such people the Father seeks to be His worshipers.
God is spirit, and those who worship Him
Must worship in spirit and truth."

—John 4:23-24—

NINETEEN

The Way into the Holy Place

In the chronicles of the restoration of the church, it will be noted that a time came when the saints ceased being satisfied with their song services, when the deepest longings of their hearts ascended beyond the sounds of shouts and hand clapping – a transitional time when pure worship began to carry them into the actual presence of God.

We Are the Temple of God

Our pursuit of God would profit from a brief study of the book of Hebrews. This book, originally written "to the Hebrews," is a message to people who were familiar with the tabernacle of God and the significance of the Divine Presence in the inner court of the tabernacle. We will be exploring the similarities between the outer and inner courts of the Hebrew tabernacle and the "outer and inner courts" of the New Testament tabernacle: *the Spirit-filled disciple*. Both have a sacred place that was created for the presence of God. And both have a prescribed way to enter the sacred presence.

Paul tells us, "Examine yourselves! Or do you not recognize this about yourselves, that Jesus Christ is in you?" (2 Cor. 13:5). Again, we are challenged, "Do you not know that you are a temple of God and that the Spirit of God dwells in you?" (1 Cor. 3:16). And again, Jesus, speaking for both Himself and God the Father, promised, "If anyone loves Me, he will keep My word; and My Father will love him, and We will come to him, and make Our abode with him" (John 14:23).

Such statements are so bold that most Bible teachers refuse to deal with them for fear of being accused of heresy. Yet, the incredible reality of God's Word cannot be altered in spite of compromise within the church. The holy meaning of the Word stands towering above men's traditions and unbelief. There is an "upward call of God in Christ Jesus" (Phil. 3:14). We must not ignore or rush past any of God's words. Rather, we encourage you to take time with this study, to dwell in it. For if you receive it properly, a door will swing open before you into the secret place of the Most High.

THE OUTER AND INNER ROOMS

There is a place in your spirit where Christ actually dwells, an abiding place where His Holy Spirit and your human spirit literally touch. You are eternally saved not because you accepted the religion called Christianity but because you have accepted the actual Spirit of Jesus Christ into your heart. Through Him you are able to come to God.

This is not merely a doctrine of faith; it is a matter of fact. This place is a holy place. We accept this truth because it is biblical. But how do we gain access to this holy place? And, once entered, is it possible to dwell there continually? The book of Hebrews provides us with an answer. In chapter nine we read, "The Holy Spirit is signifying this, that the way into the holy place has not yet been disclosed while the outer tabernacle is still standing" (Heb. 9:8).

There is a way to enter God's presence, but this way is not revealed as long as the outer tabernacle is still standing. What is this "outer tabernacle"? For the Jews, the outer tabernacle was the larger of the two rooms in the sacred tent. In this room we find the lampstand, the table, and the sacred bread (Heb. 9:2).

It was also the first room the priests entered as they ministered the daily worship service (Heb. 9:6). A second inner room was also in the tent. It is this inner room that the high priest entered just once a year (Heb. 9:7). This was the Holy of Holies, the dwelling place of God on earth. In this room dwelt His manifest presence. God did not dwell in the "outer tabernacle"; He dwelt in the inner room.

The outer and inner rooms of the Jewish tabernacle correspond to our own outer and inner natures. Our "outer tabernacle" is our soul life, constituting the view of life as seen through the mind and emotions (the soul) of man. In the outer tabernacle of our soul, our focus is outward. Worship consists of something we "perform" through a proper adherence to the ritual of our particular form of service, according to our denomination or sect. It is that part of us that keeps us in church because of duty rather than vision. It leads us by our traditions instead of being led by the Spirit.

Rarely, if ever, does one experience the actual presence of the living God in the outer tabernacle. We may be saved by faith, but by experience the presence of God seems far removed. What is experienced is a myriad of different ideas, emotionalism (or lack thereof), and much confusion concerning church order, eschatology and systems of worship. As long as man is ruled by circumstances rather than God, his "outer tabernacle" is still standing. No matter how zealous he seems, until the strength of his outer man is broken and an inner desire to worship and know God arises, the way into the holy place remains hidden.

Continuing the parallels between the Jewish tabernacle and human nature, the Bible tells us there was also an "inner tabernacle," which the Scriptures call the "Holy of Holies." This inner tabernacle corresponds to the spiritual side of man. As it was in the physical temple, so it is in the temple of flesh: the presence of God dwells in the inner tabernacle. In the physical temple, the inner tabernacle was so sacred, so holy, that great care was expended before it could be entered; no one casually entered the holy place. Into this Holy of Holies "the high priest enters once a year, not without taking blood, which he offers for himself and for the sins of the people committed in ignorance" (Heb. 9:7).

This inner tabernacle was the most sacred place on earth, for the manifested presence of Yahweh, God of Israel, dwelt in this sacred room. When we think of entering the reality of God's presence, we are immediately confronted with the depth of our sinfulness. How shall we approach God and live?

Yet, for us, the way into the holy place is not through self-improvement or any similar vain attempt. We enter the presence of God through our identification with Jesus Christ. God is not seeking to perfect us but rather to perfect our relationship with Jesus. He is our way into the holy place. He said, "No one comes to the Father but through Me" (John 14:6). Christ's expressed purpose is to bring us "to the Father." Most Christians place this promise in the hereafter. However, Jesus came to reconcile us to God in the *here and now* as well. Do not let this truth escape you! Some of the traditions we have used to define Christianity have a certain degree of deception in them, not because they are not eternally true, but because they do not accommodate the provision of God for today.

The Scriptures tell us that "through Him we ... have our access in one Spirit to the Father" (Eph. 2:18). The Word proclaims that we are "a holy temple in the Lord, in whom [we] also are being built together into a dwelling of God in the Spirit" (Eph. 2:21-22). We are God's holy temple, His habitation in the Spirit, and it is "access ... to the Father," where the Eternal One actually communes with us, that we are seeking.

But for what purpose do we seek God? We seek God to worship Him. Jesus said the Father is seeking worshipers. The worship that fully satisfies God must originate from the Holy of Holies, where the consciousness of man is awakened to the Spirit of

God. Worship does not come from any system or form of service. Rather, it is the result of having truly discovered the Almighty One in "spirit and truth" (John 4:23).

Lord, prepare my heart that it might truly be an inner tabernacle for Your presence. I present to You my secret place, where I can worship You, O God of Israel, in spirit and in truth.

Adapted from *Holiness, Truth and the Presence of God*

TWENTY

MEASURE THOSE WHO WORSHIP

At the end of the age there will be two types of Christians: those who worship in the inner court and those outside the place of intimacy.

Then there was given me a measuring rod like a staff; and someone said, "Get up and measure the temple of God and the altar, and those who worship in it. Leave out the court which is outside the temple and do not measure it, for it has been given to the nations." —Revelation 11:1-2

For whatever else this verse ultimately means, it tells us now that the Spirit of God is measuring worshipers – those individuals whose treasure is in Heaven, who abide in the inner court of God's temple. Beloved, those who truly worship God dwell in a measured and protected place.

Consider: in our world of terrors, pressures and trauma, our only refuge exists in the living presence of God. We must not accept a religion *about* God instead of the presence *of* God. If we are to truly dwell in the Divine Presence, one thing perhaps above all others will take us there: *we must become true worshipers of God.*

True Worship

Jesus taught that "true worshipers" are those who worship "the Father in spirit and truth." In other words, their worship to God flows from their heart unhindered by difficult outward conditions. "Spirit and truth" worship is *genuine* worship. Indeed, right now on Planet Earth, the Father is seeking such people "to be His worshipers" (John 4: 23).

Consider well the priority of God. He isn't seeking for us to be miracle workers or great apostles and prophets. He desires more from us than the cultivation of good leadership skills or administrative strengths. What does He seek? *He desires that we become His worshipers in spirit and truth.*

Genuine Worship Causes Us To Become Genuine Christians

If we focus on making our worship true, our Bible study, prayer, and extended service to God, whatever that may be, will also become true. Indeed, a worshiping heart floods all other spiritual disciplines with legitimacy and substance. If we bow in worship before studying God's Word, His word will plunge more deeply into our soul; our fruit will be sweeter and more enduring. If, before we open our mouths in prayer, we honor God in worship, our intercession will ascend toward Heaven on wings of unfeigned trust and expectant faith.

Worship rescues our spiritual efforts from routine, religiosity, pride and guilt; it takes our minds completely off ourselves and burrows us into the overwhelming life of God.

We have all heard teachings that God desires to have a relationship with us, and it is true. Yet, the implication is that His relationship with us is perfectly accommodating, nearly casual in its nature and mostly defined by our terms and needs. Yes, God desires that our union with Him be full and wonderful. Yet, His descent into our lives, His commitment to redeem and restore us, has another purpose: the reality of His presence transforms us into worshipers.

Indeed, worship is the evidence of a transformed life. Worship may be expressed with tears of joy or in silent awe; it may create an abiding gratitude toward God or inspire songs in the night. Regardless of the form of expression, the worship the Father seeks is absolutely meaningful. It turns our complete being toward God in love.

If, however, the idea of "worship" seems to be a strange thing, if it feels mechanical or the words expressed seem hollow (and not hallowed), it is because the soul of the individual has not first been transformed. The closer we draw to God, the more we are transformed; the greater our transformation, the more completely we respond in worship. You see, true worship deepens and matures as we walk on with God.

Recall the aged apostle John's testimony. He was in his nineties when he wrote, "We have come to know and have believed the love which God has for us" (1 John 4:16). Listen to that first phrase: *we have come to know.*

When we first come to God, by necessity we must come as we are with sin and shame. Yes, we seek to repent of our obvious sins, but the work of God is destined to go much deeper. As young Christians, we still carry attitudes of pride, ambition and fear, as well as many other sins, which cause us to misrepresent the actual nature of God to others. Though we are sinful, God does not abandon us. Instead, His work continues. His illuminating fire enters the darkened caverns of our hearts. Here, in this furnace of divine refinement, stripped of our pretenses and pride, spiritually naked, without a rag of self-righteousness in which to clothe ourselves – in this stark reality we *come to know* God's unconditional love and acceptance.

What once sounded like an impossible command, "You shall love the Lord your God with all your heart, and with all your soul, and with all your mind" (Matt. 22:37), is transformed from a law into a promise full of hope, an anticipation that He will transform all that we are and, in the process, create the praise of our lips. It is as though He says, *You shall love Me with all your heart for that is exactly how I love you, with all My heart.*

Our worship is the result of His drawing near to us; it is the effect He has upon the redeemed. Yet, it is also a choice we make. I choose worship as a way to demonstrate my trust in God when my circumstances appear hostile; I choose worship as my means of burrowing into the heart of God when all around me is in turmoil. And as I'm lifted into His presence, I am also aware that the character of my life is being measured, and it's being measured by my worship at His altar.

Lord, come into my life and fulfill Your promise of transformation. Create praise on my lips, and help me to worship You in spirit and in truth.

TWENTY-ONE

A Thankful Heart

If we will seek God and find Him, we must know what keys open the gate to God's presence. At the core of our lives, God seeks gratitude. If you think you know God but do not live your life in gratitude before Him, it is doubtful that you really knew Him in the first place. A thankful heart honors God. Often when we say we "know God," what we really mean is that we know facts *about* God. But we should ask ourselves, *"Do I truly know Him?"*

Paul warns that just knowing doctrines about God is not enough to enter eternal life. He said,

> For since the creation of the world His invisible attributes, His eternal power and divine nature, have been clearly seen, being understood through what has been made, so that they are without excuse.
>
> For even though they knew God, they did not honor Him as God or give thanks, but they became futile in their speculations, and their foolish heart was darkened.
>
> —Romans 1:20-21

A Thankful Man Is a Humble Man

Even though we may know God, if we do not honor Him as God and thank Him for ruling in our lives, our thoughts turn foolish and our minds darken. When we are in that ungrateful state of mind, every word we speak is a spark lit by hell, set to feed upon and consume our joy and hope in this world.

H.W. Beecher said, *"Pride slays thanksgiving … a proud man is seldom a grateful man, for he never thinks he gets as much as he deserves."* We should be thankful that we do not get what we deserve, for each of us deserves hell! When adversities or the small irritations of life come your way, be thankful you are not getting what you deserve!

The truth is, God's plan allows for problems so He can teach us to "rejoice always; pray without ceasing; in everything give thanks" (1 Thess. 5:16-18). The Bible tells us that these attitudes are "God's will for you in Christ Jesus" (v. 18). Are small irritations God's will? No. *Rejoicing* in the difficulty is God's will; that you remain *thankful* during the crisis is God's will.

It is obvious that the Lord does not want us to succumb to defeat, for it is His will that we "pray without ceasing." He did not say, "Accept the difficulties." He said to pray, continue to rejoice and remain vocally thankful. As you do, your circumstances will be established in victory!

This very thing happened to me during a time of great difficulty in the beginning of my ministry. I was battling with poverty, disappointment and the struggle of guiding our congregation's growth. I knew I was at a crossroads. But, as long as I thought I deserved more, I was not thankful for what the Lord had given me.

When God gives us less than we desire, it is not because He is teaching us poverty; He is teaching us thankfulness. *You see, life – real life – is not based upon what we amass but on what we enjoy.* In those very circumstances God had given me much to appreciate, but I could not see it because my heart was wrong. Once I repented and simply began to enjoy the church He had given me, my whole life changed.

God wants us to be blessed, to prosper with the real things of life. However, if we are distracted by comparing ourselves to other churches or other people, how can we appreciate what He has given us? We simply need to be grateful.

Someone once said, "*When I see a poor man who is grateful, I know if he were rich, he would be generous.*" A thankful spirit is akin to a generous spirit, for both appreciate and receive the riches as from God. When we are thankful with little, God can entrust us with much.

Out of Zion God Has Shown Forth

"The Mighty One, God, the Lord, has spoken, and summoned the earth from the rising of the sun to its setting. Out of Zion, the perfection of beauty, God has shone forth" (Ps. 50:1-2). God shines forth out of Zion. It is this God who beautifies His creation with His presence, who calls His people into covenant union. To accomplish the glorification of His people, the Lord calls, "Gather My godly ones to Me, those who have made a covenant with Me by sacrifice" (Ps. 50:5).

To make a covenant with someone is to enjoin ourselves in the most solemn bonds of unity. A covenant is more than a promise; it is the pledge of two lives to live as one. The union God seeks with us is called *a covenant of sacrifice*.

This covenant is not a ritual form of worship; it is not the Jewish sacrifice of bulls and goats. It transcends time and methodology, reaching to every soul who longs for the living God. It is a covenant of thanksgiving. He says,

> "Gather My godly ones to Me, those who have made a covenant with Me by sacrifice…. I know every bird of the mountains, and everything that moves in the field is Mine…. Offer to God a sacrifice of thanksgiving, and pay your vows to the Most High…. He who offers a sacrifice of thanksgiving honors Me; and to him who orders his way aright I shall show the salvation of God."
>
> —Psalm 50:5, 11, 14, 23

The terms of the covenant are simple: we pledge to thank Him and adore Him in everything; He pledges to shine forth from our lives in the perfection of beauty. It is a *sacrifice* of thanksgiving, for it will cost us to praise Him when we hurt. But to do so is part of our healing and the beginning of our salvation.

Begin to thank Him. Name the gifts He has given you, starting with the blessing of life itself. When we thank Him, we are honoring Him.

Today God is calling for His people to enter into a covenant bond with Him – a covenant where we pledge to live a thankful life and He pledges His life to shine forth through us. This covenant of thanksgiving is the key that shuts and bolts the door to demonic oppression in a person's life. It is a glorious gate into the stronghold of God.

Blessed Lord, I come this day to covenant with You. By Your grace, I will be thankful regardless of what my life seems. Master, I choose to worship You in my present circumstances. You have given me so much: Your Son, Your Word, Your Spirit, Your faithfulness, Your grace and Your plan for my life. Forgive me for complaining. You said that this was Your will for me: to rejoice always, to pray without ceasing and in everything give thanks. This day, I make a covenant of thanksgiving. In Jesus' name. Amen.

Adapted from *The Shelter of the Most High*

TWENTY-TWO

"This Time I Will Praise the Lord"

We cannot pass through life without getting hurt. Pain and disappointment in this world are inevitable. How we handle our setbacks, though, shapes our character and prepares us for eternity. Our attitude is the pivotal factor determining the level of our protection from strife.

Regardless of the hardships we have faced, and in spite of the mistakes we have made, the end of our lives can either be full of praise and thanksgiving or full of misery and complaint. In the final analysis, what we have experienced in life will be as rich as the desires we have had fulfilled or as painful as the things we regret.

The Bible tells us, "Hope deferred makes the heart sick" (Prov. 13:12). Deep disappointments in life have a way of never leaving us; they enter our hearts like fire and then harden into our nature like lava. Setbacks can leave us cautious about new ventures and suspicious of new friends.

Our woundedness restrains our openness. We are fearful we will be hurt again by new relationships. Gradually, unless we learn to handle heartache correctly, we become embittered and resentful cynics. We lose the joy of being alive.

The Source of Fulfillment

It is our own desires and the degree of their fulfillment that produce either joy or sorrow in our lives. Even basic desires for marriage or friends can enslave us if they consume our attention. Are these desires evil? No, but if having our desires fulfilled is the main reason we have come to Christ, it is possible our lives simply will not improve until our priorities change.

The Lord is concerned about fulfilling our desires, but to do so He must pry our fingers off our lives and turn our hearts toward Him. Indeed, the reason we are alive is not to fulfill our desires but to become His worshipers.

Personal fulfillment can become an idol; it can develop into such an obsession that we are living for happiness more than living for God. Thus, part of our salvation includes having our desires prioritized by Christ. In the Sermon on the Mount, He put it this way: "Seek first His kingdom and His righteousness, and all these things will be added to you. So do not worry about tomorrow; for tomorrow will care for itself" (Matt. 6:33-34). God wants to, and will, satisfy us beyond our dreams, but not before He is first in our hearts.

A wonderful example of this can be seen in the life of Leah, Jacob's first wife. Leah was unattractive, unwanted, and unloved by her husband. Jacob had served Laban, Leah's father, seven years for Rachel, who was Leah's younger sister. On their wedding night, however, Laban put Leah in the nuptial tent instead of Rachel. Although Jacob actually did marry Rachel a week later, he had to work another seven years for her. So Jacob had two wives who were sisters.

The Scriptures tell us that Rachel was loved by Jacob, but Leah was hated: "When the Lord saw that Leah was hated…" (Gen. 29:31 KJV). We must understand this about the nature of God: the Lord is drawn to those who hurt. "The Lord saw … Leah." What wonderful words! In the same way water descends and fills that which is lowest, so Christ reaches first to the afflicted, to fill the lowliest and comfort them.

The Lord saw that Leah was unloved. He saw her pain, loneliness, and heartache. Leah, though unloved by Jacob, was deeply loved by the Lord, and He gave her a son. Leah's reaction was predictable. She said, "Surely now my husband will love me" (v. 32).

Worse than living your life alone is to be married to someone who hates you, as was Leah. How Leah wished that Jacob would share the love he had for Rachel with her. Who could blame her? Leah's desires were justified. She had given him a firstborn son. In her mind, if the Lord could open her womb, He could also open Jacob's heart. But the time was not yet; Jacob still did not love her.

Twice more Leah gave birth to sons, and each time her desire was for her husband. She said, "Now this time my husband will become attached to me, because I have borne him three sons" (v. 34). Yet, Jacob's heart still did not desire her.

For Leah, as well as for us, there is a lesson here: you cannot make another person love you. In fact, the more pressure you place upon others to accept you, the more likely they are to reject you instead. Leah's concept of fulfillment was based on attaining Jacob's love and now her problem was worsening. Not only was she unattractive to Jacob, but also her jealousies were adding to her lack of loveliness.

Three times we read in this text that the Lord saw and heard that Leah was unloved. He had seen her affliction. Through all her striving for Jacob and her disappointment with her marital relationship, the Lord was tenderly wooing Leah to Himself.

As Leah became pregnant a fourth time, a miracle of grace occurred within her. She gradually became aware that, while she had not been the focus of her husband's love, she was loved by God. And as this fourth pregnancy drew near to completion, she drew nearer and nearer to God. She became a worshiper of the Almighty.

Now as she gave birth to another son, she said, "This time I will praise the Lord" (v. 35). She named that child *Judah*, which means, "praise." It was from the tribe of Judah that Christ was born.

Leah had been seeking self-fulfillment and found only heartache and pain. But as she became a worshiper of God, she entered life's highest fulfillment: she began to please God.

It is right here that the human soul truly begins to change and enter God's stronghold. As she found fulfillment in God, He began to remove from her the jealousies, insecurities, and heartaches that life had conveyed to her. A true inner beauty started growing in Leah; she became a woman at rest.

Likewise, we each have character defects that we are reluctant or unable to face. Others have seen these things in us, but they have lacked the courage to tell us. Both physically and personally, these flaws in our nature are what leave us anxious, threatened, and unfulfilled.

It is not counsel or classes on success or self-esteem that we need; we simply need to discover God's love for us. As we begin to praise Him in all things, we simultaneously put on the garments of salvation. We are actually being saved from that which would otherwise have destroyed us!

Disappointments and heartaches cannot cling to us, for we are worshipers of God! And, "God causes all things to work together for good to those who love God" (Rom. 8:28). If we continue to love God, nothing we experience can ultimately turn out harmful since God takes all we pass through and, in His redemptive power, works it for our good!

THE TREE OF LIFE

You will remember the verse we quoted, "Hope deferred makes the heart sick" (Prov. 13:12). The verse concludes with, "But desire fulfilled is a tree of life." As our desires are fulfilled, we are fulfilled. Since it is the fulfillment of our desires that fills us with satisfaction, the secret to a rewarding life is to commit our desires to God.

Let Him choose the times and means of our fulfillment, allow-ing the Lord to prepare us for Himself along the way. The truth is that in ourselves we are incomplete; but in Christ we have been made complete (Col. 2:10).

You say, "That's easy for you to say. You have a wonderful wife and family. You are blessed. But you don't understand my prob-lems." Yes, I do. My wonderful marriage was very difficult for the first few years. We struggled with many things in our relationship. My wife and I both came to the place where we were unfulfilled in each other. But, like Leah, we both looked to God and said, "This time I will praise the Lord." In fact, we named our second child the very name Leah gave to her fourth – Judah.

For us, as for Leah, our lives were turned around as we chose to delight in God in spite of being unfulfilled with each other. As we became His worshipers, He began to work on our hearts until we were not only more pleasing to Him, we were also pleasing to each other! What I am relating to you is the very thing that saved and blessed our marriage!

Psalm 37:4 reads, "Delight yourself in the Lord; and He will give you the desires of your heart." As you delight in God, you change. The negative effects of disappointment and grief fall off. As love and joy from God begin to fulfill us, our very souls are restored and beautified. Yes, delight yourself with Jesus and your self-destructive tendencies will actually begin to vanish. Christ will beautify your life from the inside out.

THE OUTCOME OF LEAH'S LIFE

What happened with Leah? Well, the long years came and went. In time, Rachel and then Leah died. Jacob, on his deathbed, spoke to his sons: "I am about to be gathered to my people; bury me with my fathers in the cave ... which Abraham bought ... for a burial site. There they buried Abraham and his wife Sarah, there they buried Isaac and his wife Rebekah, and there I buried Leah" (Gen. 49:29-31).

Jacob had buried Leah in the ancestral place of honor! Oh how those words, though few, say so much! They tell us that God had, in some marvelous inner way, beautified this afflicted one with salvation. After Leah found fulfillment in God, God gave her fulfillment in Jacob. Over the years, inner peace and spiritual beauty shone forth from Leah; Jacob was knit to her in love. It is not hard to imagine that when Leah died, she left smiling, with the praises of God upon her lips.

Become a worshiper of God! As you surrender your desires to Him, as you put Him first, He will take what you give Him and make it beautiful in its time. He will take what has been bent and imbalanced within you and make you stand upright in His light and glory.

Therefore, this day speak to your soul. Tell the areas of unfulfillment within you that this time you will praise the Lord!

Lord, I am a Leah, unlovely and always seeking the love of those who have rejected me. How foolish I have been. How blind. There is no love, no fulfillment in this life apart from You. You are the Tree of Life that satisfies all desires; You are the Healer of my heart. I love You, Lord Jesus. Amen.

Adapted from *The Shelter of the Most High*

TWENTY-THREE

"TELL FRANCIS
I MISS HIM"

If Satan cannot distract you with worldliness, He will overwhelm you with weariness. Indeed, how easy it is to wear ourselves out; even good works done without recharging ourselves in God can drain us of life and energy. Daniel speaks of a time at the end of the age when the enemy will attempt to "wear down the saints of the Highest One" (Dan. 7:25). God never intended for us to do His will without His presence. The power to accomplish God's purpose comes from prayer and intimacy with Christ. It is here, closed in with God, where we find an ever-replenishing flow of spiritual virtue.

Weary in Well-Doing

In the early 1970s, during the beginning of my ministry, the Lord called me to consecrate to Him the time from dawn until noon. I spent these hours in prayer, worship, and the study of His Word. I would often worship God for hours, writing songs to Him that came from this wonderful sanctuary of love. The presence of the Lord was my delight, and I know my time with Him was not only well spent but also well pleasing to us both.

However, as my life began to bear the fruit of Christ's influence, the Holy Spirit brought people to me for ministry. In time, as more people came, I found myself cutting off forty-five minutes from the end of my devotional time. On occasion, ministry to people extended into the night, and I stopped rising as early as I had.

Church growth problems began to eat at the quality of my remaining time; ministerial expansion, training younger ministries, and more counseling and deliverance crowded the already limited time I had left. Of course, these changes did not happen overnight, but the months and years of increasing "success" were steadily eroding my devotional life. In time I found myself in a growing ministry but with a shrinking anointing to sustain it.

One day an intercessor called who prayed regularly for me. He told me that during the night the Lord spoke to him in a dream concerning me. I was eager to hear what the Lord had revealed to my friend, thinking perhaps He was going to increase our outreach or maybe supply some needed finances. I asked him to tell me the dream.

What the Lord said had nothing directly to do with the projects and priorities that were consuming my time. He simply said, "Tell Francis I miss him."

Oh, what burdens we carry — what weariness accumulates — when we neglect the privilege of daily spending time with Jesus. I cried as I repented before the Lord, and I readjusted my priorities. No longer would I counsel people in the mornings. I would spend this time again with God.

I was sure I would lose some of the people who had recently joined the church. These were people who had come specifically for personal ministry. I knew I would not have the same time for them as before, but I had to make my decision for God.

The next Sunday morning I announced to the congregation that my mornings were off limits, consecrated to God. "Please," I said, "no calls or counseling. I need to spend time with the Lord." What happened next shocked me. The entire church rose and applauded! They wanted a leader who spent more time with God! They were tired of a tired pastor.

As we enter the coming days, our primary activity will be to minister to Christ. Certainly there will be increased pressures. There will also be times of great harvest and spiritual activity. No matter what circumstances surround us, we must position ourselves first and continually in the presence of God. For to miss our time with Jesus is to miss His glory in the day of His presence.

Father, it is the fragrance of Jesus, cultivated in secret, that manifests through us the knowledge of Him in every place. Forgive me for being anxious and troubled about many things, when to sit at Your feet was the only necessary thing. I choose now that better part, and gratefully receive from Your intimacy the better things which shall never be taken away.

Adapted from *The Days of His Presence*

TWENTY-FOUR

A True Worshiper

The Lord has multitudes who believe in Him, but only a minority who truly worship Him. True worshipers find their fulfillment in adoring God. The fragrance of their worship rises, not only during the scheduled times of church services but also during inconvenient times. A true worshiper will rise early before work or school; they're up before the household so they can be alone with God. Instead of being frustrated by delays, they transform difficulties and setbacks into opportunities to magnify God. You might see one of these worshipers sitting in the car next to you during a traffic jam, singing along with worship music in their car.

A true worshiper has learned the secret of worshiping God at inconvenient times.

I, too, find the Lord leading me to worship Him during inconvenient times. I might be alone writing or working on some important project when something awakens in my spirit: *I become aware that the presence of the Lord is near.* He isn't commanding me to worship; He's *inviting* me. The time of worship may be as little as ten or fifteen minutes, or it might be much longer. Regardless, I turn from what I am doing, pick up my guitar, and begin to worship Him.

Frankly, I am not a good musician; I only know a few chords. Yet as I worship, I know the King of Heaven is actually pleased with my offering. He has granted me an audience, and in some mysterious way, He causes me to feel that the sound of my worship is the only thing He hears as I'm singing.

The Invitation

I, for one, desire my worship to become all consuming. I do confess that a primary obstacle I must overcome is the inconvenient timing of His invitation. It seems like He chooses to wait until I am focused on some important project – something He actually wants me to complete. Or it might be late at night when I am almost asleep that the opportunity to worship draws near.

The very fact that I have responded, in spite of the "inconvenience," actually refines and sweetens my worship. Indeed, when

I worship in our Sunday service, I admit I can be carried by the sound of the music and the participation of others around me. I am in an atmosphere of worship, so my praise may actually be something imparted to me by others and not purely my own. However, when He comes at an inconvenient time, my response reaffirms that my worship is real and that God truly is first in my life.

What is also a great pleasure to me is that, given such short notice, He does not expect from me a large production. As wonderful as Sunday worship services are, He is not looking for a professional song service, just something real from my heart.

Another blessing is that often my wife will hear me worshiping and, without fail, join me. As I worship, I'll soon notice a voice singing alongside me in the background. She's as absorbed as I am in the presence of God. It doesn't matter what she had been doing, she loves to bow before God; that, too, sweetens our worship.

PRAYER AND WORSHIP

There is a difference between prayer and worship. Prayer is an appeal to God based on our needs and the needs of our world. The world is filled with people, each with heartfelt and urgent requests that are welcomed by our Father in Heaven, and they are each heard in the throne room of light. However, worship is not the articulation of our needs; it is the consummation of our love. It is what we offer to God regardless of the status of our needs.

Recall the gospel account of the ten leprous men who cried to Jesus for healing. After the Lord answered their prayers and healed them, they all went their way. One, however, stopped and "turned back, glorifying God with a loud voice, and he fell on his face at

His feet, giving thanks to Him" (Luke 17:15-16). Full of gratitude to Christ, this man returned to bow in worship before God. You see, many people will pray, multitudes will find answers, but few will return to Him in worship.

Beloved, if worship flows genuinely from our hearts, the Lord will repeatedly invite us into His presence. His invitation will approach the doorstep of our souls quietly. It will come disguised as a simple desire to love Him. If we follow this desire, it will lead into the presence of God.

As we worship Him, He will grant us inner strength and peace. As we come with thanksgiving, He will refresh us with His love and joy. Let us delight in the privilege of becoming true worshipers of God, even when the opportunity comes at an inconvenient time.

Lord Jesus, forgive us for being so easily distracted. Deliver us from the bondage of the physical world; liberate us to enjoy the powers of the spiritual world. Intoxicate us with Your presence. Make us God-addicts who cannot go through our day without more of You in our lives.

TWENTY-FIVE

ARMY OF WORSHIPERS

W hen the Scriptures refer to the "heavenly host," we usually think of "choirs of angels." The word *host* in the Bible meant "army" (Josh. 5:13-14). It is an important truth: the hosts of Heaven are worshiping armies. Indeed, no one can do warfare who is not first a worshiper of God. One does not have to penetrate deeply into the Revelation of John to discover that both

God and the devil are seeking worshipers (Rev. 7:11; 13:4; 14:7, 11). Time and time again the line is drawn between those who "worship the beast and his image" and those who worship God.

In the last great battle before Jesus returns, the outcome of every man's life shall be weighed upon a scale of worship: in the midst of warfare and battles to whom will we bow, God or Satan?

Yet, while this warfare shall end in the establishment of the Lord's kingdom on earth (Rev. 11:15), we must realize the essence of this battle is the central issue in our warfare today.

The Central Issue in Tribulation Is Worship

Will we faithfully worship God during satanic assault and temptation? True worship must emerge now in the context of our daily lives, for no man will worship through the great battles of tomorrow who complains in the mere skirmishes of today.

You will remember that the Lord's call to the Israelites was a call to worship and serve Him in the wilderness (Exod. 7:16). Indeed, when Moses first spoke of God's loving concern, we read that the Hebrews "bowed low and worshiped" (Exod. 4:31). But when trials and pressures came, they fell quickly into murmuring, complaining and blatant rebellion. Their worship was superficial, self-serving and conditional – form without a heart of worship.

This same condition of shallow worship prevails in much of Christianity today. If a message is given that speaks of the Lord's great care for His people, with eagerness do we bow low and worship. But as soon as the pressures of daily living arise or temptations come, how quickly we rebel against God and resist His dealings! The enemy has easy access to the soul that is not protected by true worship of the Almighty! Indeed, the Lord's purpose with Israel in the wilderness was to perfect true worship, which is based upon the reality of God, not circumstances. The Lord knows that the heart that will worship Him in the wilderness of affliction will continue to worship in the promised land of plenty.

Without true worship of God, there can be no victory in warfare. For what we bleed when we are wounded by satanic assault or difficult circumstances is the true measure of our worship. You see, what comes out of our hearts during times of pressure is in us, but it's hidden during times of ease. If you are a true worshiper, your spirit will exude worship to God no matter what battle you are fighting. In warfare, worship creates a wall of fire around the soul.

PROTECTING YOUR HEART THROUGH WORSHIP

Most of us understand the basic dynamics of the human soul. We have been taught, and rightly so, that the soul is the combination of our mind, will and emotions. Generally speaking, when the enemy comes against the church, he targets any of these three areas. We must see that the protection of these areas is of vital importance in our war against Satan.

To further illuminate the nature of this battle, let us add that, in addition to the mind, the will and the emotions, the soul is also made up of events and how we responded to those events. Who we are today is the sum of what we have encountered in life and our subsequent reactions. Abuses and afflictions hammer us one way, encouragement and praise inflate us another. Our reaction to each event, whether that event was positive or negative, is poured into the creative marrow of our individuality, where it is blended into the nature of our character.

What we call memory is actually our spirit gazing at the substance of our soul. With few exceptions, those events that we remember the most have also shaped us the most. Indeed, the reason our natural minds cannot forget certain incidents is because those events have literally become part of our nature.

Our soul, with its strengths and weaknesses, has been shaped by how well or how poorly we handled our past experiences. When Scripture commands us to not look back and to "forget … what lies behind" (Phil. 3:13; Luke 9:62), it is saying we must undo the consequences that have come from our unchristlike reactions. With God, this is not impossible, for although the events of our lives are irreversible, our reactions to those events can still be changed. As our wrong reactions to the past change, we change. In other words, although we cannot alter the past, we can put our past upon the "altar" as an act of worship. A worshiping heart truly allows God to restore the soul.

All of us receive a portion of both good and evil in this world. But for life to be good, God, who is the essence of life, must reach into our experiences and redeem us from our negative reactions. The channel through which the Lord extends Himself, even into our past, is our love and worship of Him.

"And we know that God causes all things to work together for good to those who love God" (Rom. 8:28). The key for the fulfillment of this verse is that we become lovers of God in our spirits. Bad things become good for "those who love God." When we are given to loving Him, all that we have passed through in life is washed and redeemed in that love. Bad becomes good by the power of God.

Therefore, it is essential to both the salvation of our souls and our protection in warfare that we be worshipers. The ship that safely carries us through the storms of adversity is worship.

Psalm 84 expresses in praise to God the wonderful effect worship has upon the soul. "How blessed is the man whose strength is in You, in whose heart are the highways to Zion! Passing through the valley of Baca [weeping] they make it a spring; the early rain also covers it with blessings" (vv. 5-6).

If you are "ever praising" God (Ps. 84:4), your worship of God will transform the negative assault of the enemy into "a spring" of sweet refreshing waters. No matter what befalls a worshiper, their "valley of weeping" always becomes a spring covered "with blessings." You cannot successfully engage in warfare, nor pass safely through the wilderness of this life, without first becoming a worshiper of God.

Worship Is the Purpose of Creation

We were created for God's pleasure. We were not created to live for ourselves but for Him. And while the Lord desires that we enjoy His gifts and His people, He would have us know we were created first for His pleasure. In these closing moments of this age, the Lord will produce a people whose purpose for living is to please God with their lives. In them, God finds His own reward for creating man. They are His worshipers. They are on earth only to please God, and when He is pleased, they also are pleased.

The Lord takes them farther and through more pain and conflicts than other men. Outwardly, they often seem "smitten of

God, and afflicted" (Isa. 53:4). Yet to God, they are His beloved. When they are crushed, like the petals of a flower, they exude a worship, the fragrance of which is so beautiful and rare that angels weep in quiet awe at their surrender. They are the Lord's purpose for creation.

One would think that God would protect them, guarding them in such a way that they would not be marred. Instead, they are marred more than others. Indeed, when they pass through times of extraordinary crushing, in the midst of physical and emotional pain, their loyalty to Christ grows pure and perfect. And in the face of persecutions, their love and worship toward God become all-consuming.

Would that all Christ's servants lived lives so perfectly surrendered. Yet God finds His pleasure in us all. As the days of the kingdom draw near and the warfare at the end of this age increases, those who have been created solely for the worship of God will come forth in the power and glory of the Son. With the high praises of God in their mouths, they will execute upon His enemies the judgment written against them (Ps. 149). They will lead as generals in the Lord's army of worshipers.

I surrender, Lord! I give myself to You and enlist in Your army of worshipers. I choose to give You my praise and increase Your shelter around me with the worship I give to You. You are my purpose for living.

Adapted from *The Three Battlegrounds*

BOOKS
BY FRANCIS FRANGIPANE

THE THREE BATTLEGROUNDS. *Revised Edition:* An in-depth view of three arenas of spiritual warfare: the mind, the church and the heavenly places.

THE POWER OF ONE CHRISTLIKE LIFE. The prayer of a Christlike intercessor is the most powerful force in the universe, delaying God's wrath until He pours out His mercy.

THE POWER OF COVENANT PRAYER. Gain the victory over the effect of curses. The section on persevering prayer is a must for anyone serious about attaining Christlikeness. The second part is the conclusion of a teaching on spiritual protection. Powerful insights on the nature of curses and how to walk in spiritual victory and freedom. (Formerly titled *The Divine Antidote*). *Published by Charisma House.*

AND I WILL BE FOUND BY YOU. The essence of *And I Will Be Found By You* is a living promise from God. If we genuinely, from our heart, pursue the Lord, He promises He will meet us. Francis calls the church to a focused season of seeking God. We must have more of God, and if it is God we desire, it is God we shall find!

THIS DAY WE FIGHT. We cannot be passive and also win the war for our souls. Pastor Frangipane exposes the disarming that occurs when we accept a passive spirit into our thoughts. The passive spirit seems innocent, yet it causes us to stop seeking God, ultimately rendering us defenseless against spiritual attack and the weaknesses of our flesh. This is essential reading for the overcoming church. *Published by Chosen Books.*

THE SHELTER OF THE MOST HIGH. Francis gives trustworthy, biblical evidence that in the midst of all our uncertainties and fears there is an available shelter from God to shield us. Once you have found this place, nothing you encounter can defeat you. This is a revised and expanded version of *The Stronghold of God. Published by Charisma House.*

HOLINESS, TRUTH AND THE PRESENCE OF GOD. A penetrating study of the human heart and how God prepares it for His glory. *Published by Charisma House.*

A HOUSE UNITED. Few works of the enemy are as destructive to the body of Christ as a church split. Once a wedge is driven into the heart of a congregation, the result is usually bitterness, grief, even hatred among those who are called to live together in love. This is an expanded version of the book *It's Time to End Church Splits. Published by Chosen Books.*

THE DAYS OF HIS PRESENCE. As the day of the Lord draws near, though darkness covers the earth, the out-raying of Christ's presence shall arise and appear upon His people!

WHEN THE MANY ARE ONE. How the Christian community – driven by grace, unified in love, and activated by prayer – can bring revival and change. This is a revised and expanded version of *The House of the Lord. Published by Charisma House.*

TO ORDER MINISTRY RESOURCES:
go to www.arrowbookstore.com

FOR TEACHINGS AND CONFERENCE SCHEDULE:
go to www.frangipane.org

IN CHRIST'S IMAGE TRAINING
ONLINE CORRESPONDENCE COURSE
Curriculum developed by Francis Frangipane

In Christ's Image Training offers four opportunities for enrollment in Level I training each year: January, April, July and October.

LEVEL I: Certification offers four foundational tracks: Christlikeness, Humility, Prayer and Unity. Completion time is six months.

LEVEL II: Growing in Christ offers further online teaching by Pastor Francis and other national church leaders. Completion time is three months.

LEVEL III: Facilitation and Commissioning provides spiritual equipping for those preparing for ministerial opportunities.

ON-SITE Impartation and Focused Training offers a three-day seminar which can be taken by attendance or via CD/DVD albums or MP3/MP4 downloads.

Available in Spanish!
Contact us at spanish@inchristsimage.org for more information.

IN CHRIST'S IMAGE TRAINING MATERIALS
BASIC TRAINING MANUALS

This study series pulls together four key areas of this ministry: Christlikeness, Humility, Prayer and Unity. Perfect for leadership teams, prayer groups, Bible studies and individuals who are seeking to possess a more Christlike life. It is strongly recommended that these four manuals be read in sequence, as each study is built upon the truths found in the preceding manuals.

For enrollment fees and detailed information, go to ICITC.org.

A special thanks to Charisma House for
allowing us to use messages from the following books:

The Shelter of the Most High by Francis Frangipane
(www.strang.com; Lake Mary, FL: Charisma House, 2008).
Used by permission.

When the Many Are One by Francis Frangipane
(www.strang.com; Lake Mary, FL: Charisma House, 2009).
Used by permission.